TRIMINGHAM – A SINGULAR VILLAGE

Roger Kirk

was born in 1944 and lived in Trimingham from 1945 until 1963.
He was Educated at the Paston School, Hornsey College of Art and
Middlesex University, and graduated in 1967 with a B.Sc. (Soc).
He worked for Williams Deacons Bank in Curzon Street, Mayfair, then in
the Trustee Department in the City of London. He played drums in a
moderately successful rock band. He moved into the oil industry with
Phillips Petroleum Company and then Conoco for the next 20 years.
Changing career in 1987, he returned to the art world as a self-employed
artist, painting in watercolour, oils and acrylic, then took up writing in
2000. In addition to *'Trimingham, A Singular Village'* he has written two
novels and co-written a drama for TV. He is presently writing another
novel and researching a play for radio, based upon a tragic event in
Great Yarmouth.

TRIMINGHAM –
A SINGULAR VILLAGE

Roger Kirk

Larks Press

Published by the Larks Press
Ordnance Farmhouse, Guist Bottom, Dereham,
Norfolk NR20 5PF
01328 829207
Larks.Press@btinternet.com
Website: www.booksatlarkspress.co.uk

Printed by the Lanceni Press,
Garrood Drive, Fakenham, Norfolk

May 2007

British Library Cataloguing-in-Publication Data
A catalogue record for this book is available
from the British Library

ISBN 1 904006 37 4

Introduction

I spent most of the first eighteen years of my life in Trimingham, a small seaside village on top of the highest cliffs on the North Norfolk coast.

Despite the challenges presented at the time by poor housing, rationing, the lack of basic services and the numerous other rigours of post-war rural life, Trimingham is a place that I recall with fondness. However, as I grew up through the late 1940s, the 50s and into the 60s, it was clear that Trimingham was seen by many as rather different from other villages. Certainly this was not an unusual view, and it was often vociferously expressed. One or two of the critics and gainsayers actually knew where Trimingham was, although, predictably, many had never been to the village. Some admitted to passing through, on their way to somewhere altogether more interesting.

On leaving Trimingham for London in 1963 I found it unsurprising that virtually no one had heard of the village. Few knew Mundesley or Overstrand. Many struggled with Cromer. Most had heard of Norwich or Norfolk, but an alarming number had no idea where they were.

Following father's demobilisation from The Royal Welsh Fusiliers in 1946, I moved with my parents, Henry and Lucy Kirk, into a tiny rented cottage at the top of Middle Street in Trimingham. I was not yet two at the time. We remained in that cottage until the early 1950s, when, urgently in need of more room following the birth of my brother Anthony, we moved to one of four newly completed council houses at the far end of the village, on the Cromer Road. There I lived until the age of 18 when I left home for London and Hornsey College of Art. I have had occasion to visit Trimingham frequently since that time as my parents continued to live in the village until their deaths, and my brother lives there still.

I have wondered from time to time whether there really was, or is, anything different about Trimingham. Having grown up there I knew something of its past, both ancient and more recent. Off the top my head I knew of several items of interest that would probably repay investigation. If there *was* anything particular, was it a comparatively recent development or were its roots in an earlier time? I decided to investigate, to see whether there is, or ever was, anything truly singular about Trimingham.

Roger Kirk

Contents

1. A Small and Quiet Village

There is no mention of Trimingham in the Domesday Book. An article that first appeared in the *Norwich Mercury* at the end of the 19th century and was reissued in *Norfolk Churches - Hundred of North Erpingham* by T. Hugh Bryant in 1900, spoke of a township called *Tryminga* that was part of Earl Warren's lordship of Gymingham or Gunningham at the time of the survey in 1086. It was held by 'Rathi, one free man,' and the population of 77 was made up of 23 sokemen (peasant farmers) and 54 bond tenants, of which 12 were villeins, 40 were bordars and 2 were slaves. It is unlikely that there was a church within the settlement at the time.

The article continued that a Crown Pleas Roll in 1286 referred to the following:-'The jury find that all free tenants of the soke of Gymingham, consisting of eight villages, viz:- Gymingham, Knapton, Sutreppes, North Reppes, Trunch, Sydestrond and Trimingham, used to follow the sheriff's turn twice a year with four men and the constable of the village, which John de Warren withdrew to the damage of the King of 16s. a year.' I count only seven villages, perhaps Moneslie made the eighth.

Centuries later, in 1829, in *A General History of the County of Norfolk,* John Stacy noted that 'the following doggerel memoranda of the approximity of these places are often in the mouths of the common people - Gimingham and Trimingham, Knapton and Trunch, Northrepps and Southrepps, lie all in a bunch.' There is no shortage of people still ready with the old rhyme to celebrate the locality today.

The *Norwich Mercury* article continued that in 1316, under Nomina Villarum - Treasurer's Remembrancer of the Exchequer is the following reference;- 'Trimingh'm en' Sydestrond. Roger de Reymes, Wms. De Weyland.'

In 1319 a fine was levied, whereby 'John de Warren, Earl of Surrey, settled on Thomas, Earl of Lancaster, this advowson of Thrymingham with the Hundreds of Gallow and Brothercross, the Manors of Gymingham and others. From this time it became parcell (sic) of the

Honour of Lancaster,' and eventually passed to John of Gaunt, Duke of Lancaster and to Henry IV.

The soke of Gimingham was a functioning economic and jurisdictional entity with an elaborate organisation. A reeve presided over eight annually elected wickeners, who were responsible for collecting rents and other dues owed by the tenants. A fragment from the parish records shows that as late as 1656 the wickener for Trimingham collected rents and dues from members of the families of Clipperton, Newman, Cubitt, Thirst and Clarke.

There are many 'inghams' in this part of Norfolk. William Tylney Spurdens M.A. concluded in his *Manuscript Collection relating to the County of Norfolk* in 1853, that in the case of Trimingham, 'ingham' meant literally a meadow, home or dwelling. The final 'ham' possibly indicated a separate or detached abode. He felt unable to form any conjecture about 'Trim' and concluded that it had been arbitrarily imposed. A more recent expert, Professor Ekwall, opted for 'the homestead of Trymma's people'.

By the end of the 19th century Trimingham was a small village of some 645 acres with a population of 200 or so. Lord Suffield was Lord of the Manor, although most of the parish belonged to J. H. Buxton Esq.

*

Singular or not, Trimingham has frequently been described as a small and quiet village, or a hamlet, situated on lofty cliffs. Despite an increase in housing and population in recent times the description is arguably apt today.

> 'We're on the road to nowhere, everyone passes by,
> Nobody comes to Norfolk unless there's a reason why.'

Even its staunchest champion might concede that the rhyme could apply equally to Trimingham; but it hasn't always been the case. On occasion people came in numbers. Some came on pilgrimage, drawn by spiritual need or to give thanks. Many came to relax, to enjoy the beach and the scenery and recharge their batteries. Others were seduced by newspaper articles and the opportunity perhaps to rub shoulders with the great and the good at the better-known resorts close by. Yet others came on at least two occasions, dispatched in response to national emergency.

Situated beside the North Sea, the entire parish stands within an area acknowledged to be of outstanding natural beauty. Part of the parish has been designated a conservation area since 1975. The highest cliffs on the North Norfolk coast and the wide sandy beach are recognised as a site of special scientific interest.

4

For centuries parish land has been lost to coastal erosion and a significant portion of the village now lies within an area designated at risk. There have been some boundary changes, but today the parish extends to roughly 518 acres.

A visitor's eye might be caught by the gleaming white dome at the radar station on Beacon Hill, but for those that knew the Crown and Anchor Hotel the forlorn site where it once stood is equally arresting. It is not unlike the gummy gap left after a tooth extraction. The church, the old farmhouses, the flint cottages and some of the recent barn conversions are undeniably picturesque. Other constraints obviously influenced some of the building over the last half-century or so although most recent construction work has been carried out sympathetically. However, Trimingham remains a ribbon village situated on the B1159. Despite the 'B' designation it is the main coast road between Great Yarmouth and Cromer.

Given the nature and volume of traffic today, negotiating Trimingham's narrow streets can be something of a challenge. The steep banks and cobble walls are unforgiving, but this is not a new problem. The Parish Council campaigned to widen the road and erect warning signs as early as the 1920s. Signs were erected but the road is no wider. Concentrating on these hazards it is easy enough to pass through the village without comment. Charming as it is, situated midway between the fashionable watering places in west Norfolk and the holiday beaches and dunes in the east, there is perhaps little to excite the average visitor.

What of the local people or those connected with Trimingham? Some have caused comment, or have been recognised for one reason or another outside the parish. Sir Thomas Fowell Buxton owned land in Trimingham. A renowned social reformer, he was instrumental in bringing about the abolition of slavery in Britain's colonies. According to Howard Temperley (Emeritus Professor of History, University of East Anglia) it was Buxton who was foremost in the campaign, and not William Wilberforce, who is most frequently recognised as the prime mover. After leaving parliament in 1837 Buxton retired to Northrepps, but the family continued to play a significant part in Trimingham life from the mid 19th century for the next hundred years or so.

The priests who claimed possession of the head of St John the Baptist were certainly well known since for a time Trimingham church became a place of pilgrimage. Centuries later the deeds and reputations of those who cleared mines from the cliffs and beaches and those who operated the various radar facilities spread far beyond the parish boundary.

5

Trimingham has also harboured the odd bad egg from time to time, one or two of whom featured in the local and national press. There have been tales of smugglers and certainly for much of the 19th century H. M. Preventive Service maintained a significant presence. In 1783 Benjamin Royal and the crew of a smuggling cutter from Hunstanton plundered Trimingham, taking bedding, butter and cheese before setting sail for Flushing. In 1787 the authorities seized 150 casks of foreign spirits at Trimingham, but it wasn't just alcoholic wares that came ashore. Owing to the outrageous level of duty, there was a thriving trade in smuggled tea. Even today there persist rumours of tunnels running from the cliffs into Middle Street and as far as Grove Farm in Gimingham, but I suspect that there is little truth in these tales.

The initials of one Edmund Nurse, born in Trimingham in 1769 can be found on a gable at Weybourne Mill. Nurse also built Kelling postmill in about 1820.

In his *Royal Illustrated History of Eastern England*, A. D. Bayne found that Trimingham 'was formerly a much-neglected parish.' Bayne continued that by 1856 the Buxtons had 'restored the church, built new cottages and a school and celebrated the good work by such a harvest home as the parish had never witnessed before.'

Trimingham from the air. The photograph was taken before March 1988 when the Crown and Anchor Hotel was destroyed by fire. Erosion of the cliffs is clearly illustrated.

2. Fragrance, Invigoration and Inspirational Views

A few miles to the west of Trimingham, Cromer was an established watering place by 1785. By the turn of the century Mundesley, 2½ miles to the east, had also gained something of a reputation as a place for bathing. The poet William Cowper visited Mundesley in 1795 and 1798. Suffering with melancholia, it was hoped that these visits to the seaside would prove beneficial to his health.

'The cliff is here of a height that is terrible to look down from,' he wrote. Of a visit, almost certainly to Marl Point at Trimingham, he was moved to record the following. 'At two miles distance on the coast is a solitary pillar of rock that the crumbling cliff has left at the high water mark. I have visited it twice, and found it an emblem of myself. Torn from my natural connections, I stand alone and expect the storm that shall displace me.' Cowper's visits certainly made an impression although whether they had the desired effect is open to conjecture.

Marl Point, photograph by P.G.H.Boswell in the 19th century.
This was probably the 'solitary pillar of rock' that the poet,
William Cowper, visited in the late 18th century.
Courtesy of the Norfolk County Council Library & Information Service

Since they shared many of the qualities that made Cromer and Mundesley successful, the villages between them, Overstrand, Sidestrand and Trimingham, became popular too. To a degree they were also beholden to the 'Poppyland' writings of journalist and poet Clement Scott. The son of a London vicar, Scott arrived in Cromer in 1883, sent by the *Daily Telegraph* to look at the potential of the resort. Dismayed by the crowds and failing to find lodgings, he eventually fetched up at Mill House in Sidestrand. There he struck up an enduring friendship with Louie Jermy, the miller's daughter. He wrote about the area for some time, publishing in 1886 his newspaper articles in a work entitled 'Poppyland.' The volume included a poem 'The Garden of Sleep,' about the ruined church at Sidestrand. The poem was soon set to music and sung in many a Victorian drawing room. Well known in theatrical circles, Scott introduced a number of famous and influential people to this part of the North Norfolk coast. A visit to Poppyland became as crucial a part of the summer season as attendance at Cowes Week and Royal Ascot.

The BBC broadcast a film entitled 'Poppyland' in 1984. During filming they built a replica of the ruined Sidestrand church tower on the cliff top at Trimingham, to serve as a location. Ford Granadas and Sierras stood bumper to bumper in the field behind the Pilgrim Shelter. The locals had never seen anything like it. One of the actors was heard to mutter from deep inside a thick tweed coat that he had filmed all over the world and never been as cold as he was on that cliff top at Trimingham.

Cromer was the favourite resort and stamping ground of a number of wealthy banking and Quaker families. The Gurneys, Barclays, Buxtons, Birkbecks, the Hoares and Lord Suffield of Gunton Park all frequented the town. Until about 1870 Cromer remained a select resort for the nobility and gentry.

Faced at that time with an agricultural slump and falling incomes the landowners turned their attention to developing their coastal landholdings. They had seen the railway to Hunstanton built in 1862 at modest cost. From the beginning it made a profit. Lord Suffield, then Chairman of the East Norfolk Railway, was a prime mover in the development that followed.

Despite the aim of many of the villages on the North Norfolk coast to remain exclusive, the coming of the railways made the area increasingly accessible. The Duke of York, the Churchills, the Empress of Austria and other luminaries visited. They brought in their wake reporters and camp followers. Increasing numbers of a new and rising class found that they too could save for a sojourn at the seaside. Chief clerks, skilled craftsmen and shop managers arrived with their families to breathe the sea air, bathe, take in the view and perhaps mingle for a moment with the gentry.

Overstrand was a small fishing village no more than a short cab ride from Cromer and a number of the well heeled built houses and seaside cottages there. The publisher, Daniel Macmillan, and Barings the bankers visited. Sidestrand was little more than a hamlet of flint cottages with the Hoare family in residence at Sidestrand Hall.

Trimingham gained favour as a holiday resort. In 1902 a visitor reported that 'the hamlet is becoming popular with holidaymakers, chiefly on account of its fine beach, good bathing, and the walks along the cliffs.' In the Crown and Anchor the village possessed an admirable hotel with convenient camping grounds between it and the cliffs. Many local people offered accommodation. One could arrange an apartment, full board or bed and breakfast. Beacon Hill and the highest cliffs in the county afforded visitors inspirational views both out to sea and inland. The air was fragrant and invigorating and the surrounding countryside was rich with woodlands, bracken and flowers.

The Crown and Anchor Hotel
(Photograph by kind permission of North Walsham Historical Society)

It was even possible to buy souvenir china, made in Stoke on Trent. I have seen two examples, a small vase and a miniature cheese dish and cover. Both bear the name Trimingham and a coat of arms depicting among its heraldic devices a rather dashing tramp steamer set against an unfeasibly blue sea and sky.

Trimingham souvenir pottery.

For a time Trimingham flourished as a holiday resort. However, it failed to develop. Today, with the exception of Sidestrand next door, the village bears little resemblance to any of its neighbours. Despite an increase in population, the age structure and composition of which is not significantly different from North Norfolk in general, Trimingham has never developed like Mundesley or Overstrand and other seaside villages further afield.

In 2001 the population totalled 370, nearly 100 more than 50 years earlier and exactly double the 185 souls of a century before.

In 1831 the parish had 353 people, but numbers had dropped to 222 a decade on. The 1831 level would not be equalled for another 165 years. The population of the village fell considerably between 1854 and 1861. Cholera, influenza, diphtheria or something of that ilk must have been visited on the parish in 1858 when there were fifteen burials, thirteen of them children under the age of 16. Three of those to die that year were Susanna Kirk (5), John Henry Kirk (3) and Robert Kirk (3), all my forbears.

Since 1901 the numbers have risen, other than in the 1920s when the population dropped by 53 (20%), and again in the 1950s when there was a fall of 46 (17%). The decline in the 1920s coincided with agricultural unrest and the general strike. The fall in the 1950s may well have been due to nothing more than a reduction in RAF personnel.

Today there are few amenities in the village. There is no shop, Post Office, pub or school and the playing field is a comparatively recent manifestation. The railway is long gone and, with so much reliance on the car, the bus service is limited.

The beach, once accessed from as many as five pathways now has no practical access from within the village. In the past a significant number of villagers made a living as fishermen. At present no commercial fishing takes place and the prospect of any return to this activity looks bleak.

Fishermen Tom and Theo Clarke mending nets on the cliffs

Use of the beach today tends to be restricted to the very fit or the seriously determined, since there is no easily negotiable access to the sands from within the parish boundary. Other than for Woodland Leisure Park at the western extremity of the parish and Trimingham House Caravan Park just outside the eastern boundary, there are limited recreational

**Theo Clarke, Henry Kirk, Tom Kidd, Tom Clarke and Proosian Deary
inspect the contents of a net on Trimingham beach.**

facilities for locals or holidaymakers. It would be naive however to believe
that there do not exist those who are very happy with the absence of the
worst excesses of seaside development, all too evident elsewhere. The lack
of derelict petrol stations, tatty cafés, slot machine emporia and the
hawkers of gewgaws and tat is not all bad.

3. Zeppelins and Spies

Towards the end of 1914 there was a strong rumour that the north-east coast of Norfolk was the most likely landing place for a German invasion. The county became crowded with troops as the Army established gun positions round the coast from Weybourne to Mundesley.

On November 18th 1914 approximately 150 men of the Middlesex Yeomen arrived in Trimingham. Two officers, three troopers and five horses took up residence at the Rectory while the main force camped out in the west of the village. The weather was bitterly cold and life was hard for the troops. Each night they were engaged on cavalry patrols along the coast.

They interned a German resident from Trimingham House following a rumour that signals had been seen to ships out at sea. Rumours of spies were rife at the time. The authorities took the threat of a Christmas invasion so seriously that the Yeomen were obliged to shiver in their trenches each night throughout the festive season.

By Christmas Day the Germans had carried out three aeroplane attacks that confirmed their belief that England's air defences were ineffective. The enemy concluded that given the right weather there was little to oppose a successful airship raid.

On January 19th 1915, two Zeppelins (L3 and L4) crossed the North Sea from just north of Hamburg. They were bound for the Humber and the north-east coast. A third Zeppelin (L6) left Nordholtz near Cuxhaven for the Thames estuary. Under the command of Fregattenkapitan Peter Strasser L6 suffered engine trouble and icing and had to turn back.

Commanded by Kapitanleutnant Hans Fritz, Zeppelin L3 crossed the coast between Horsey and Happisburgh. After almost colliding with the church spire at Martham it headed for Great Yarmouth. There it dropped eleven bombs in a little over ten minutes, killing two people and causing much damage. The Zeppelin reportedly left Great Yarmouth in a north-westerly direction, following the coast round to the Runtons before heading out to sea.

Zeppelin L4 crossed the Norfolk coast near Bacton at approximately 7.55 p.m. The Commander, Kapitanleutnant Magnus von Platen-Hallermund was convinced that he was south-east of Grimsby. The airship passed over Trimingham as it followed the coast round to Cromer, which it over-flew without the crew realising that the town was below. After dropping a flare and two incendiary bombs near Sheringham the Zeppelin circled out to sea. It crossed the coast again near Holme and continued by way of Hunstanton, Heacham and Snettisham on a rather uncertain route to King's Lynn. There it dropped eight bombs in fifteen minutes, causing a good deal of damage and two fatalities. After the raid L4 headed east across country to leave by way of Great Yarmouth. Three Zeppelins were seen early the following morning over Dutch islands on their return journey. It is thought that L6 may have flown out to meet the returning L3 and L4.

The Rector of Trimingham, Rev. R. C. Page recorded in the Register of Services that both Zeppelins had been heard passing over the village that night. He also noted that the people of the village seemed very calm and indifferent to those killed at King's Lynn and Great Yarmouth.

Not a single shot was fired at the Zeppelins during the raids. However the lesson was learned and East Anglian defences were strengthened. There were more rumours of spies and secret agents. Theories and suspicions abounded that spies using car headlights had guided the airships. There was a report of a man in West Norfolk seen in the back of a car with a muffler round his head. He had a 'fair moustache and looked like a German.'

On March 21st 1915 the Rector held a service in Trimingham church for the London Mounted Brigade. There were further sightings of Zeppelins. On June 6th 1915 one was spotted about 12 miles out to sea off Trimingham. Col. Douglas Jones was entertaining wounded soldiers from North Walsham Hospital at the Rectory at the time.

During the late summer the village put on two concerts. The school was filled to overflowing on both occasions and over £10 was donated to the hospital and other good causes. Three more Zeppelins flew over the parish on October 13th. A year later on October 1st 1916 a further Zeppelin passed over Trimingham at about 10.00 p.m. The Bacton searchlight failed to find it.

Norfolk lost almost 12,000 souls in World War I. For some reason the county's losses appear proportionally higher than anywhere else in the country. One man out of every nine aged between 18 and 41 was killed or missing.

The east window in Trimingham church.
Photo: Courtesy Simon Knott

On November 11th 1918 the war came to an end. The Rector sent messengers throughout the parish calling the people to a service of thanksgiving at the church at 7 o'clock that evening. Over 100 people gathered for the service.

At a War Memorial meeting in the village on May 2nd 1919, Rev. R. C. Page stated that many other villages had been quick to erect memorials to those lost during the war. He thought that Trimingham would probably be criticised for tardiness. However, he remarked that the parish was different from others in that nearly all of the inhabitants were tenants of J.H. Buxton and all owed a great deal to him.

Four alternatives were considered as a fitting memorial; an east window for the church, an organ screen, a peal of bells - three to be added to the existing one, or a north porch. A more secular element pressed for a new parish room. Two committees were formed, one to investigate the east window and the other to consider the parish room. A leaflet was broadcast throughout the village inviting the residents to subscribe to the War Memorial Fund.

Trimingham Church War Memorial Fund.

'I promise to subscribe to:-
1. The stained glass window.
2. Church Room, estimated cost £275.'

The stained glass window won the day. It was unveiled on August 10th 1920 as a memorial to the following local men who lost their lives. Lt Sidney Bosanquet. Pte Bertie Copeman. Pte R. Brown Pardon. Maj. A. Oliver Lash. Pte A. C. Olley. Capt. Andrew Buxton. Pte Hayward Payne. Lt Cpl C. Farrow. Pte Bernard Cubitt. Cpl Bertie Olley.

The Rector, Rev. R. C. Page completed a further memorial, a tablet bearing a carved wooden panel depicting Major Lash, his late brother-in-law, at the beginning of his fatal charge across No Man's Land.

Even though the Great War was over, throughout the early 1920s the country as a whole suffered much dislocation and misery. Worldwide ten million soldiers had died and seventeen million were wounded, of whom five million would be forced to live out the remainder of their lives as chronic invalids. In the parish of Trimingham the loss of ten young men from a total population of 250 was devastating.

**The 1914-18 War Memorial in Trimingham Church,
carved by Rev. R. C. Page.**

4. E-Boat Alley and other hazards

Just prior to the beginning of World War II, Trimingham was doing rather well. Rev. Arthur Buxton of the Church of all Souls, Langham Place, London was the principal landowner. John Bright farmed Beacon Farm; Christopher Harrison was at Hall Farm and the Pages worked Church Farm. The main crops were wheat, oats and barley. Matthew Bullimore was road foreman. Edith Harrison kept a boarding house at Highlawns and Mrs W. F. Lamb ran Bar Haven. Sarah Ellen Pearson owned the shop and teashop in Church Street. Ernest William Purdey also kept a shop and Post Office at The Cobbles. In the hands of G. W. Risebrow the Crown and Anchor Hotel had Bed and Breakfast available from 4s. 6d. He also advertised reasonable weekend charges, use of a garage and a bowling green. Plumbley & Gaze, coal merchants were based in the railway station yard. George Clarke was the fish merchant and a number of fishermen worked off the beach. There was a thriving holiday trade and Trimingham was flourishing.

It was not to last. The onset of another war brought significant change.

★

At the beginning of the 2nd World War the army mined much of the coast of Norfolk to protect the country from invasion. They also built pillboxes and barricades, dug trenches and anti-tank ditches and rigged bridges for demolition. If there were an invasion, broadly the plan was to hold the enemy as long as possible on the beaches before withdrawing to fallback positions based on the rivers Ant, Bure and Wensum.

East Anglian soldiers from the 18th Division (Territorials) and a workshop section of 251 Field Park Company spent much of the summer of 1940 on these activities. They built pillboxes at Trimingham, Sheringham and in South Norfolk and they ferried mines to the beaches for the sappers. These weapons were B (Beach) Type C anti-tank mines, each roughly 14 inches in diameter and weighing about 45 lbs. The mines required only to be placed in position and the detonators attached.

At Trimingham (unlike other locations) the mines were laid on the cliffs. There was also a plan to mine the strip of land on the very cliff top, reportedly to approximately 100 feet back from the cliff edge. This strip was fenced off but in the event the mines were never laid there. Farmer Chris Harrison had to breach the fence in order to harvest his barley.

The first bombs to fall on Norfolk were dropped at West Raynham at 12.35 a.m. on May 25th 1940. Thirteen high explosive bombs fell in the fields north-east of the aerodrome. There were no casualties and there was no damage to property.

It wasn't until November that Trimingham experienced its first bombing. Inexplicably the enemy dropped three incendiaries on a plantation on the cliff top. More bombs were dropped on the parish as the war progressed. Bizewell Farm and the Keeper's Cottage at the end of Buck's Heath Lane were hit. A stick of bombs fell in a line across the fields between the Keeper's Cottage and the railway station.

The Gamekeeper's Cottage on the Buxton Estate, c1920.

The Germans attacked the railway line with parachute mines, targeting the troop trains that ran between 11 p.m. and 1 a.m. The final bomb to be dropped on Norfolk was at Swanton Morley aerodrome on March 20th 1945. Trimingham got off lightly.

Ironically, since it lay directly between Germany and England and was the scene of much hostility, the east coast was not a theatre of major military operations. World attention was elsewhere, focused on the

English Channel, Dunkirk and on the Atlantic convoy and U-boat conflicts.

At the beginning of the war the shipping lanes off the east coast were extremely busy, mainly with colliers bearing coal from the north-east to the Thames estuary and London. The convoys followed a fixed route. Between Sheringham and Aldeburgh the route was two-lane, enabling convoys to pass each other safely in the dark and hopefully cause a degree of confusion to the enemy.

In May 1939 Trimingham set up an ARP Reception Centre at the school. Mr J. Kidd was Officer in Charge. The Recording Officer was Mrs Seago and Food Supply Officer was Mr Stevens. Mr Lamb became Road Traffic Officer and Special Constable. They obtained stretchers and other kit and set up a decontamination centre at Ingleside. The parish made arrangements for the collection of salvage. The Sea Scouts collected waste paper and a dump for scrap was set up on Mr Lamb's property at Bar Haven.

On September 1st 1939 more than 2,000 children were evacuated to North Norfolk. Two coaches arrived at the school bearing evacuees from Dagenham. The children were placed in homes in the village.

The army deposited an old Churchill tank on the cliff top for use as a target. They placed a caravan and sentries in the Watch House wood. The Local Defence Volunteers, later re-named the Home Guard, met regularly in the Pilgrim Shelter. The new force came into being on May 14th 1940. Within 48 hours approximately 6,000 men signed up in Norfolk. By the end of the month the number had swelled to 30,000. They were mostly men either too young or too old for the regular army, or those in reserved occupations.

The enemy overran Holland in May 1940, raising fears of an invasion of the East Coast. Outmoded Coastal Artillery fortifications were expanded and 6-inch guns were introduced at Mundesley (Battery No. 197) behind the Grand Hotel and Weybourne (Battery No. 324.)

German E-boats sank two ships near Happisburgh sands on the night of September 4th 1940. E-boats were fast diesel-powered vessels equipped with torpedoes and mines. The activity of these vessels was such that the Great Yarmouth section of the convoy route became known as 'E-boat alley.'

November 1940 saw an isolated victory against the E-boats when one was rammed and sunk off Southwold. It was the first confirmed destruction of an E-boat. However on Friday March 7th 1941, E-boats destroyed 7 merchant ships as two convoys passed each other off Norfolk. 42 ships in two columns made up the southbound convoy FS29. It was escorted by a destroyer and a corvette. The northbound convoy FN26 contained 29 vessels in two lines and had three ships escorting. During the action SS *Kenton* (1047t), en route from Poole to Tyneside, SS *Corduff* (2345t) en route from London to Hull and SS *Boulderpool* (4805t) going from London to the Tyne were lost off Cromer. The following day SS *Togson* (1547t) en route from Blyth to London also perished. One of the vessels foundered off Trimingham and was later used by the RAF as a target for bombing practice. A Blenheim bomber engaged in this activity crashed at Hall Farm at 1.43 p.m. on September 22nd 1941. Too low after dropping smoke bombs on the wrecked ship, the aeroplane clipped the cliff top and came down in Gray's Yard, the field between the cliff top and Hall Farm. Rev. Page, who saw the crash, and Frank Reynolds, who was working in the next field, hurried to the scene. Arthur Hunt, the head man at Hall Farm, and his sons were working in the barn at the time. On hearing the noise they ran across the road towards the stricken plane. The bomber blew up before anyone could reach it. The crew of three was killed.

The shortage of petrol was taking its toll by 1942 and the District Council took over the collection of salvage. In August there was a parish meeting to organise fire-watching during the harvest. Eighteen parishioners volunteered to take watch between the hours of 11 p.m. and 4 a.m.

In 1943 the railings encircling two graves in the churchyard were removed for salvage. By this time the dumping of scrap at Bar Haven was completely out of hand with all kinds of rubbish being left. Following the threat of prosecution the site was promptly cleared up and no action was necessary.

The Parochial Church Council approved a Social Club in connection with the church for the forces stationed in the parish. The YMCA was asked to furnish and equip the old schoolroom for the venture, but when it came to light that the club was intended to be all male, the PCC withdrew its support.

A further fatal air crash occurred in the parish on April 8th 1944. At 1.10 p.m. a Liberator bomber came down in the paddock behind Bizewell Farm. Four of the crew were killed. Another six were injured and taken to Cromer Hospital.

Local men Bertie Barker, Walter G. Seago and Reginald Buck lost their lives during the 1939-45 war. They are commemorated in the church by a panel carved by Rev. R. C. Page.

In April 1946 the Parish Council discussed victory celebrations for the village. The programme entailed taking the children to Cromer by charabanc to see a display, followed by tea in one of the halls. The council contributed £5 towards the cost. In March the following year the council agreed to express its appreciation to the tradesmen, the postal authorities and others who had provided such excellent service to the parish under very trying conditions throughout the conflict.

Immediately after the 2nd World War the parish was desperately short of accommodation. Men who had left the parish single were now returning, several of them with wives and children. Many had no alternative but to move in with family or rent rooms. There was a need for new council housing. A survey of unoccupied property turned up two houses at Cliff Farm, furnished and unoccupied for 9-12 months each year. A wooden bungalow (Windy Ridge) was unoccupied, and there were two cottages and a large outbuilding at Three Ways in Middle Street that were largely unused. The Chapel was also empty. The Council considered acquiring Highlawns and converting it to flats.

A full year later there were still many families living in rooms. The Parish Council approached Erpingham Rural District Council (ERDC) and requested that unoccupied property in the village be requisitioned, but this seems to have come to nought.

5. 'Danger. Mines. Keep out.'

By 1944 the threat of invasion was receding. In January that year No. 4 Bomb Disposal Company, Royal Engineers began clearance of some of the minefields in Norfolk. Immediately men began losing their lives in this risky endeavour. Between 1944 and 1953, a total of 26 men died in mine clearance on the beaches of Norfolk.

Great Yarmouth, Caister, Winterton, Horsey, Waxham, Happisburgh, Trimingham, Weybourne and Holkham all saw fatalities. Two Royal Engineers lost their lives on May 6th 1953 on the beach at Trimingham. The *Eastern Daily Press* reported the accident on Saturday May 9th 1953.

> 'One does not mourn brave men; one salutes them,' declared the Dereham District Coroner (Mr L. H. Allwood) at an inquest at Trimingham on the two soldiers who lost their lives on Wednesday in the minefield. That morning a mine was detected and marked with a cone about two fifths of the way up the cliff. Both men saw this cone. In the afternoon an explosion was heard. Those investigating found a crater with a body lying some 50 yards away. Parts of another body were found over a wide area. The coroner said that the men were on a particularly dangerous job which they faced with cool-headed courage, and they earned the gratitude of the people of the village and Norfolk.

He continued that they died just as much for their country in 1953 as if the accident had happened in 1943.

Others too died in the Trimingham minefield. An exploding mine killed two boys in January 1943. A third boy survived the incident. Civilian Ben J. Payne, aged 65, also lost his life to a mine on the cliffs while hunting rabbits.

While mine clearance went on apace on other beaches it became obvious that clearance at Trimingham would be extremely difficult. Maps of the minefield that survived the war were useless. Cliff falls and erosion had changed the cliff and beach significantly from what existed when the mines were laid. Things looked so bleak that an Act of Parliament in 1946 authorised the sealing off of the minefield at Trimingham for perpetuity.

Despite the beach closure, in April 1946 the Parish Council received an application from a Mr Coleshaw for a stand on the beach from which to offer pony and donkey rides. The council informed the optimistic Mr Coleshaw that the beach was still under military control.

The successful clearance of other Norfolk beaches prompted the village to make representations in 1947 that Trimingham beach be re-opened. The village sent a petition to the Secretary of State for War advocating clearance of a 200-yard gap in the minefield opposite the church. A number of villagers believed that there was no risk on the beach at that point.

Rev. Page, the former Rector, knew a safe path to the sea. He had been in the habit of going through the minefield each morning to bathe more than 200 times before the police stopped him. In spite of the many contributions that the Rev. Page made to the village this fact is almost invariably the first thing about him that a local will tell a visitor.

In August 1947 the Secretary of State for War responded to the petition. The sweeping of approximately 2,000 yards of beach had yielded 30 or so mines in one week. Ominously, further mines were found the following week in areas previously swept. In view of this and other expert evaluation the minister refused to accept the risk of removing existing restrictions.

In 1949 Sam Cullum from Middle Street received a medal from the RSPCA for rescuing a dog from a dangerous area of the cliffs. The council also sent Mr Cullum a letter of appreciation.

By 1950 a barbed wire fence still straggled along the cliff top above the minefield. Every few hundred yards a large red notice-board hung on the wire. Each one bore the warning 'Danger. Mines. Keep Out.'

Some village people approached the Parish Council to seek compensation for loss of trade and amenities. The Chairman responded that it was not a matter for the council. Individuals were advised to submit their claims to the War Department.

In 1951 the Parish Council took offence at certain articles about the mines in the local newspaper and the parish magazine. The council considered them to be misleading. Certainly the article in the local paper was colourful and emotive.

'MINES STILL KEEP AWAY THE HOLIDAY-MAKERS,' it boomed; 'Trimingham's Anxious Query.' Reference was made to 'Forbidden Golden Sands' and 'Vanished Industry.' The article mentioned the belief of less optimistic residents who feared that the mines, already in situ for ten years, would be there for another fifty. Trimingham, it continued, was a seaside village whose prosperity was decided by its holiday amenities. Before the war it was very popular. Campers pitched their tents near the Crown and Anchor Hotel in their scores and almost every house in the village took in visitors, while the local inhabitants retired to stout garden sheds for their sleep. The hotel catered for hundreds.

Mrs K. R. Yaxley, wife of the licensee of the Crown and Anchor lamented the passing of the days when Trimingham was full of families enjoying the golden stretch of now forbidden sand, and the subsequent loss of more than half of the hotel catering business.

Before the minefield was laid several longshore boats set out from Trimingham. 'They are not there now. Two-thirds of Trimingham's livelihood, it is reckoned, has been destroyed by the presence of mines, and Trimingham exists now solely as a cliff-top farming village.' The newspaper article may have been a little vivid but it was essentially accurate.

In September 1952 the village learned that it might finally lose the unenviable distinction of possessing the last minefield of the war. Ironically this intelligence came by way of a letter to Mundesley Parish Council. They had written directly to the Secretary of State for War expressing concern about mines from Trimingham being washed up on Mundesley beach. Discussions and meetings in August resulted in a letter from the Commander of the Bomb Disposal Unit proposing an attempt in the summer of 1953 to clear the ¼ mile of minefield nearest Mundesley. He hoped that experience gained would help in an assessment of the dangers and practicality of clearing the remainder of the minefield. The work would be classed as top priority. Mundesley Parish Council was most gratified that its concerns had received such prompt attention.

There was a flurry of excitement during November 1952. Bomb disposal personnel were seen driving old railway lines into the beach at the Mundesley end of the minefield. It turned out that they were doing no more than replacing the old barrier and notices that had been washed away by the sea.

It was a mine washed up on Great Yarmouth beach that caused the authorities to have a change of heart. Although harmless it had the effect of focusing attention on the situation at Trimingham. The next mine to frolic with the bathers might lead to an altogether different outcome.

Work to clear the minefield eventually got under way in 1953. A Bomb Disposal Unit comprising an officer, a warrant officer, six men, ten civilians and seven German ex-POWs began work full time on searching for the mines. By October the unit had cleared about half a mile of cliff face of over 100 mines. A local newspaper spoke of several thousand mines being cleared in the next three years. This was not only an inaccurate assessment of the number of mines planted but a wildly optimistic view of the near term future of the minefield.

Sweeping the cliffs for mines 1950s
Photo: Courtesy Archant Norfolk Photographic

As predicted, cliff falls and erosion made detecting and clearing the mines extraordinarily difficult. The project became a major engineering exercise. A man with a small hand-held mine detector on the cliff face could sweep in one afternoon no more than a 3-foot wide strip from top to bottom of the cliff. Another method, originally devised to locate bombs was adapted for detecting mines. Aluminium pipes driven into the beach in a pattern around a suspected mine enabled a device to be lowered into each tube. The detector was capable of penetrating up to six feet. Every find had to be exposed and its nature determined.

Later large pumping appliances washed down the cliffs and armoured bulldozers cut away portions of the cliff face. Once mines were located and exposed the Unit disposed of them either by a charge detonated by fuse or through an electric cable. The fuse was the preferred method for mines exposed on the cliffs.

In November 1953 the Unit tried to demolish a large area of cliff by detonating ten high explosive charges at the cliff base. Pared away at the foot by bulldozers the cliff had become too dangerous for men or machines to work on or beneath. Three newsreel companies with cine cameras recorded the event. It was a partial success, as only a quarter of the expected cliff fall took place.

A Sapper of the Bomb Disposal Unit on a safety rope using a mine detector on the cliffs at Trimingham.

Visiting the minefield in April 1957 Lieut. General C. F. C. Coleman, G. O. C. Eastern Command saw for himself the difficulties encountered in clearing the mines. He learned that it was necessary to re-sweep each cleared area at three-monthly intervals. The beach profile could change, sometimes scouring or building as much as five feet overnight. The tides ensured that no equipment, even heavy bulldozers, could be left at low level. Erosion of the cliffs and shifting topsoil were an ever-present danger.

In November 1957 the Bomb Disposal Unit again demonstrated the problems that they faced, this time to the national and local press. The Unit conducted the visitors along a safety lane more than two miles in length at the foot of the cliffs. In four years they had cleared roughly half of the minefield. They took great pains to point out that the remaining half would not necessarily be cleared in the next four years.

The continued deprivation of use of the beach brought complaints in 1958 from people unable to let rooms in the village. The Parish Council once again requested that the Bomb Disposal Unit clear a strip of beach before the following summer.

In the six years of operation to 1959, the Unit lifted between 50 and 75 tons of scrap metal from the beach. The villagers raised another petition seeking a path down to the beach and requesting that coastal

Detecting mines on the beach at Trimingham.

defence work be put in operation. On receipt of a very detailed letter from the Colonel of the Bomb Disposal Unit, the Parish Council decided not to support the petition.

On occasion the Bomb Disposal Unit sounded a siren to indicate that an explosion was imminent. Sometimes they drove through the village with the hand-cranked siren wailing from the back of a truck. Certain of the village women opened their windows to save the glass but this was not always effective.

As children we knew better than to take liberties with the cliffs or the minefield. Parents had harangued every child in the village on the subject. We had all experienced the bang and the shock wave from an exploding mine and knew that they were not to be taken lightly.

Walking on the cliff tops to the west of the Watch House wood one afternoon in 1960 I heard shouts from the beach below. As I looked over the cliff edge there was a huge explosion. I didn't see it but I felt the shock wave, much too close for comfort. A distorted piece of metal the size of a saucer landed about thirty feet behind me. It must have travelled well over 300 feet from the site of the explosion.

January 1963 saw hopes raised that part of the beach might be reopened during the summer. A military spokesman was quoted as saying, 'Although the beach has not been entirely cleared yet, it is hoped that certain sections will be re-opened by the season.' But hopes were dashed again by the end of June. The War Office told ERDC that after reviewing the matter carefully with the Home Office it had 'regretfully decided on the evidence of the continuing risk,' not to re-open the beach to the public. Over 500 mines had been found by this time and although fewer were being found each year the War Office was certain that 'an indefinite number' still remained in the area.

In October 1965 ERDC agreed to a proposal by the Ministry of Defence to re-open the Trimingham/Sidestrand beach to the public. The number of mines sown on the cliffs in 1940 was not known but an exhaustive search of the records had shown that the total did not exceed 1,000. Mines accounted for since 1953 totalled 528. It was estimated conservatively that a further 300 would have self-detonated or been washed out. The remaining 100 or so undoubtedly posed a hazard, but much of the cliff in which the mines were originally sown no longer existed, having eroded at the rate of about seven feet a year. It was concluded that although there was no certainty that the remains of the original cliff was clear of mines, the risk on the beach was no greater than that on other beaches in the area.

Bert Hazell, North Norfolk's Labour MP, was taken on a tour of inspection of the beach during November 1965. Days later, as he was being informed in the House of Commons that the Ministry of Defence had decided to allow access to the beach, a mine was detonated only 50 yards from where he had walked. It was only the second mine found in the minefield since 1963. The Under Secretary of State for Defence stated that he would no longer be justified in denying the public access to the beach. The cliffs however would have to remain closed.

The saga of Trimingham minefield wasn't quite over though. In March 1966 it came to light that a clerical oversight at the Ministry of Defence kept the beach closed to the public for six months longer than it need have been. A limited clearance certificate for the beach should have been issued the previous October.

The eastern end of the village and the vicinity of the Pilgrim Shelter were the initial locations planned for providing new access to the beach. After difficulties with these sites an alternative was sought behind the Crown and Anchor. A member of the public wondered whether wooden steps, built and maintained by voluntary labour and removed in the winter might provide a solution.

Towards the end of July 1966 there was gathering optimism that the beach might still re-open that summer. This was despite ERDC's lack of success in negotiations to acquire cliff top land off the Loop Road for provision of beach access. The Ministry of Defence then agreed that the public could use the existing access behind the Bomb Disposal depot.

On Monday August 1st 1966 the barriers finally came down. It was 26 long years since the beach had last been open to the public. The people of Trimingham and Sidestrand could once again enjoy their beaches, but only if they went first to Overstrand to the west or to the Bomb Disposal depot at Vale Road in the east. Negotiations by ERDC to acquire cliff top land had reached deadlock, and the cliffs in the vicinity of the Loop Road were found to be far from suitable for a way down to the beach.

So Trimingham finally lost the distinction of possessing the last restricted beach in the country. I talked recently to Mr Leslie Stean, one of the civilians who worked at clearing the minefield. He quite enjoyed the work, he said, and he spoke warmly of the jolly parties that the Bomb Disposal Unit put on over the festive season. The worst experiences that he could recall were the several occasions on which he lost his boots in the sloughs on the cliffs. 'Oh,' he added, 'and the odd occasion when I had to help carry a live mine up the cliff.'

On May 2nd 2004 on the cliff top at Mundesley the Royal Engineers and others erected and dedicated a permanent memorial to all of the men lost in mine clearance on the coast of Norfolk.

★

I have been interested of late to see the Trimingham minefield described in Mundesley as 'the Mundesley minefield'. The Trimingham minefield comprised that area of the cliff and beach located geographically between Sidestrand and Mundesley, which was mined at the beginning of the 2nd World War and remained closed to the public from 1940 until 1966. Mundesley beach was free of mines and open to the public for most, if not all of that time.

6. Cat and Mouse

During the 2nd World War the Royal Navy set up a radar station at Trimingham. Designated a 'Y' service station it began operating in May 1941, from an outlook on the cliff tops. WRNS personnel billeted at Highlawns manned the post, using direction-finding aerials to monitor radio signals as they attempted to locate the source of enemy transmissions.

The Outlook on the cliff top at Trimingham

These operations were quite separate from the coastal defence radar station that the army established on Beacon Hill in late 1941. The purpose of the new Station No. 65 was to detect E-boats and low flying enemy aircraft. It operated on a 10cm wavelength and was designated a 'K' station to distinguish it from first generation 'M' stations that worked on one metre wavelength.

The chain of radar stations that had been in existence up to that point provided only limited help to the Navy and shipping. Just before the end of 1941 a new and potentially superior system was introduced. Trimingham became one of the first Chain Home Extra Low (CHEL) radar stations on the east coast. CHEL made possible the location of small objects vertically down to sea level at 15 miles distance. It brought within range the E-boats that plagued the convoy route.

During 1942 and 1943 responsibility for all coastal early warning stations passed to the RAF. By the end of the war the radar station at Trimingham was equipped with a Type 54a radar with a transmitter located directly below a circular dish mounted on a 200 foot tower. Standing on the crest of Beacon Hill behind Beaconhill House, this was the Trimingham mast or pylon. Located some 226 feet above sea level and 203 feet high itself, the pylon was a well-known landmark, visible for miles around.

Trimingham also had the distinction of being chosen as the site of one of the first three 'Oboe' stations. 'Oboe' was the codename given to a radar navigation aid that assisted bombers in the location of enemy targets in Europe. A sophisticated guidance system, 'Oboe' was used by pathfinder aircraft, usually Mosquitoes, to pinpoint bombing targets. The system utilised two ground stations, one code-named 'Cat' and the other 'Mouse.' Either station could be used as the 'Cat' or the 'Mouse' depending on the target location. Trimingham was operating as a 'Cat' station by December 1942. 'Mouse' was located at Walmer in Kent. These were very specialised radar stations and by March 1945 only six were in operation.

At the end of the war the radar station occupied about 7½ acres in three fields either side of the Mundesley Road. By the late 1940s the wartime radar network had become inadequate and in 1950 a plan was approved to upgrade the UK's early warning system. It aimed to address the faster speeds of jet aircraft and provide protection for radar personnel by placing control and reporting centres in bunkers. This was the Rotor plan under which Trimingham became a Centrimetric Early Warning (CEW) station. Additional land was acquired on the southern edge of the site. The Type 54 radar was modified and three height-finding radars and a surveillance radar were installed.

In 1951 the Parish Council heard, not entirely accurately, that the RAF would be opening a camp at the Beacon and that certain houses in the village would be requisitioned by the Air Ministry.

At Beacon Hill an R1 type underground bunker was built to house the reporting centre. A standard single-level bunker, access was by means of a bungalow-like guardroom. Construction called for the excavation of a huge hole in the hillside and the casting *in situ* of the R1 reinforced concrete bunker. As a boy I was one of several who leaned on the sagging fence at the roadside and watched first the excavation and then the construction work for the bunker. We goggled at the sheer size of it. The entire world seemed to be made of sand.

The main structure was complete by March 1952 but the dog-legged tunnel leading to the entrance was still open at that time. Just over a year later the bunker had been covered with earth and the bungalow guardroom completed. The bunker was constructed by Peter Lind at a cost of £300,000 for the technical facilities and £200,000 for domestic facilities. The station came on line in 1953.

In phase two of the Rotor programme Trimingham was selected as the site of the first production Type 80 search radar, a new and more powerful apparatus. It was installed in 1954 but owing to teething problems not handed over to the RAF until April 1955.

During the 1950s the RAF established a sizeable camp on the Cromer Road in Mundesley. It provided living quarters, workshops and transportation facilities for personnel working at the radar station. The influx of personnel was of limited benefit to the village of Trimingham however. RAF men visited the Crown and Anchor hotel and Bar Haven Tea Shop but the camp was on the wrong side of the radar station to bring prosperity to the village.

RAF vehicles speeding through the village became a concern, causing the Parish Council to correspond with the Commanding Officer from time to time. In March 1957 the CO gave orders that RAF vehicles were to limit their speed through the village to 20 mph. They had to address the problem again in 1959.

Bar Haven, later known as Grey Stones. The tea rooms and the miniature golf course were popular with RAF personnel from the Radar Station.

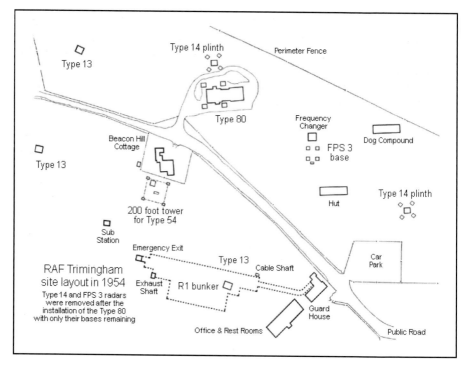

Trimingham Radar Station. Site Layout.
Courtesy of Nick Catford

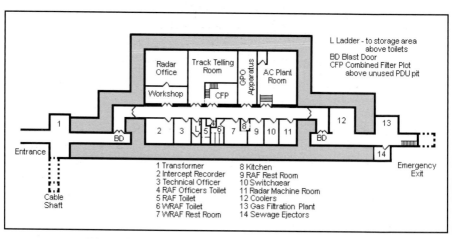

Plan of Trimingham Radar Station R1 Bunker
Courtesy of Nick Catford

The Rotor scheme was of short duration. In 1956 a new plan was put forward. Increased airspeeds and air defence missiles made it necessary for radar to identify hostile aircraft at even greater distances. Trimingham continued in its CHEL role and as a CEW station, but with American long-range radar installed. It had a range of 200 miles. Fewer personnel were required and a substantial reduction was made, from 246 to 86.

Little is known of the station through the 1960s and 70s, although by February 1st 1961 it had closed and by 1965 much of it was dismantled. All of the radar arrays were removed except for the Type 54. A sale of miscellaneous furniture and equipment took place in 1966 and the pylon was removed during the summer of 1969. By 1981 the guardroom had been converted into a private dwelling.

Demolition of the pylon at Trimingham Radar Station 1969
Photo: courtesy of Archant Norfolk Photographic

The RAF re-occupied the site in the late 1980s and a fully mobile Marconi Type 91 'Martello' radar unit was installed. It was operated by 432 Signals Unit and controlled from the R3 underground control centre at RAF Neatishead. The unit usually comprised 7 trucks to move the radar equipment and a further 8 vehicles to carry the unit's general stores when on the move.

The facilities in the late 1980s were designed to house the radar unit and its support vehicles and crew while in this temporary static position. The guardhouse was retained and converted to crew accommodation, offices and a mess. The mounds were shaved back to the concrete roof of the bunker and a new grass mound built up. The Type 91 radar was parked on the highest point on the site and the mobile control cabins and support vehicles were stationed on the lower road. Adding prefabricated shelters strengthened the perimeter defences.

In May 1987 the Type 91 radar was sold to the Turkish Ministry of Defence and replaced by a Type 93. By December 1997 the unit was being converted to a full time static role, mounted on a permanent setting within the Kevlon dome visible on the site today. The gleaming white dome that now stands in place of the old pylon is nowhere near as tall but is equally impressive, especially on a bright day in the sunshine. At its largest the radar station occupied about ten acres, situated either side of the B1159 coast road. The northern side of the road appears derelict today, but the southern side is still occupied.

★

During the war the RAF created a very hush-hush specialist radio unit, No. 80 (Signals) Wing. Its purpose was to chart and calibrate the navigational radio signals of Luftwaffe bombers and then by 'bending' them send the bombers off course, away from cities and other strategic targets. Such a site was in operation in Trimingham by 1941. Located on rising ground about 200 yards from the radar station the site comprised five or six huts dotted about a field. Each hut contained a transmitter or two, connected to a mass of tall wireless aerials.

The crews had to be particularly careful when they were on air on dry, frosty nights. They were pumping out so many kilowatts that anything metal induced current. Just touching a door handle could be hazardous.

After the local coastguard showed them a safe passage down the cliffs some of the operators visited the beach, particularly after a bad attack on the offshore convoys. After one such visit they smoked recovered Craven 'A' cigarettes for months. Apparently some of the train crews got to know the 'beam-benders' too, and threw coal for their fires from the locomotives.

★

On February 21st 2006 the *Daily Mail* and the BBC television news reported that in recent weeks a number of cars had suffered electrical and electronic problems as they passed the radar station. It was reported that engines cut out, lights flickered or died, electric windows jammed and dashboards went haywire. The MOD said that it was investigating these complaints, but that the facility was 'operating legally' and that there were 'no guarantees (that) the Trimingham radar is the cause of the reported incidents.'

7. The East End

There are a number of ways to approach Trimingham. Landfall from the sea is possible but not without hazard. In early times any water-borne approach would have caused some excitement at the beacon on Beacon Hill. Evidence of later attempts that came to grief can be found both on the beach and in the churchyard.

Arrival by air is feasible, but again not without risk. Zeppelin commanders failed to spot the difference between Humberside and Norfolk and since the beginning of the 2nd World War one of the principal purposes of the radar station on Beacon Hill has been to discourage uninvited visitors arriving by sea or air.

A third option, arrival at the local station by rail, was once popular but has not been possible for more than half a century. Tunnelling, a fourth alternative, is plainly out of the question except for smugglers.

From the East the more conventional approaches are by way of the B1159 coast road from Mundesley, or if one feels strong, the ascent of Gimingham hill. Alternatively one could try negotiating a 'quiet lane' from Gimingham or Southrepps. However travellers should beware. Traversing a quiet lane one may very well be confronted by pea viners, combine or potato harvesters or other agricultural equipment that will surely impede progress. Also at certain times of the year these lanes become no more than a single track, often breached by flood, shingle bank, sandbar, or mud. A coxcomb of grass growing down the middle of the road can shake the firmest belief in what might lie ahead. The recent 'quiet lane' signage has led to some disquiet in certain circles. There are fears that we might yet see parts of North Norfolk turned into a theme park.

Leaving Mundesley on the B1159 the rough track of Vale Road on the right leads to the old Bomb Disposal Unit site and one of only two currently viable accesses to Trimingham beach. Further up the hill the mound of Mundesley reservoir is still visible although it is no longer in use. As far back as 1899 the people of Mundesley considered their prospects as a resort seriously compromised by the lack of clean water. To rectify matters they sank a 100-foot well and piped water to the reservoir.

Map of the East End of Trimingham

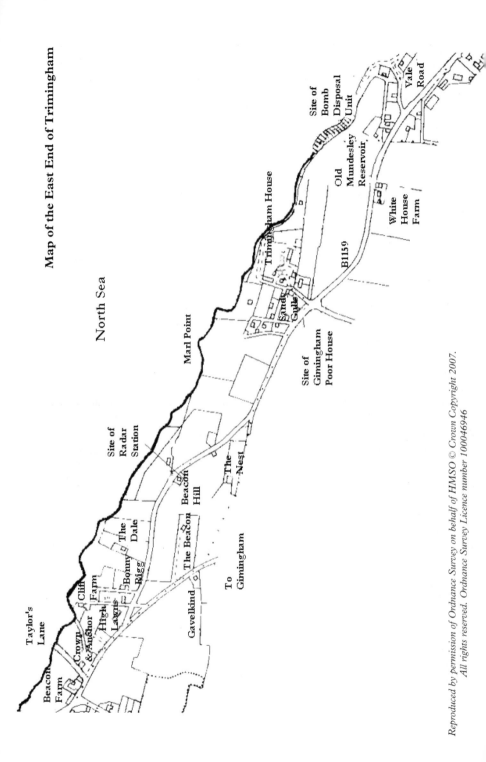

North Sea

Taylor's Lane

Beacon Farm

Crown & Anchor

Cliff Farm

High Lawns

Bonny Rigg

The Dale

Site of Radar Station

Beacon Hill

The Beacon

Gavelkind

To Gimingham

The Nest

Marl Point

Site of Gimingham Poor House

Sandy Gulls

Trimingham House

B1159

Old Mundesley Reservoir

Site of Bomb Disposal Unit

White House Farm

Vale Road

By February 1908 all existing properties in Mundesley were connected to the water system. It's a pity that Trimingham didn't follow suit. Nearly fifty years more would pass before its parishioners would be connected to a water main.

Moving on towards Trimingham, White House Farm stands on the left with its 2nd World War pillbox still in evidence. Another pillbox once stood on the cliff edge behind Trimingham House. Its remains can still be found on the beach below.

Trimingham House is no more. Now the site of a Caravan Park, the facility actually stands in Gimingham. The Gimingham Poor House once stood on this site. Built in 1805 it was one of two Poor Houses altered at a cost of about £1,500 and adopted by the Erpingham Union. The Gimingham house served nine parishes, (Gimingham, Knapton, Mundesley, Overstrand, Northrepps, Southrepps, Sidestrand, Trunch and Trimingham) and had room for 260 souls or more. In 1831 Mr George Rix and his wife were the Master and Matron, responsible for the 68 inhabitants. At the 1841 census John and Mary King were in charge. They and their three staff oversaw 61 inhabitants. The second Poor House was located at Sheringham. It too served nine parishes, in the west of the Union.

A substantial dwelling by the name of Sandy Gulls was built in the vicinity of the old Union House. Sandy Gulls boasted six bedrooms, a garage, a bungalow, two tennis courts, a paddock and approximately one acre of glebe land. When it was purchased in 1920 by William Herbert Case for £1600, both water and the telephone were laid on. The telephone, the number of which was No. 17 Mundesley, was apparently located in the gentlemen's lavatory. As late as the end of the 18th century a track ran west along the cliff top from Sandy Gulls to the vicinity of Cliff Farm.

The B1159 up to the radar station remains as narrow as ever with unforgiving banks on either side. The comparatively recently built East Rising Farm stands on the seaward side of the road. The Nest lies back from the road on the left on land once known as Beacon Field and owned by one John Golden.

Having bought part of the 20 acres of land for £80 in 1906, a Civil Engineer by the name of Andrew Miller Alexander probably built The Nest in 1908/10. Constructed almost entirely of wood, part of the original structure is thought to have been manufactured by Boulton & Paul. Similarities exist between The Nest and Mundesley Sanatorium, which opened on February 2nd 1899. Both are rare surviving late 19th century

The Nest, constructed almost entirely of wood in the early 1900s

pre-fabricated timber-frame buildings. Alexander is thought to have been involved in the building of both. The Alexander family is buried in Trimingham churchyard to the east of the chancel.

On to Beacon Hill, which, although frequently said to be so, is not the highest point in Norfolk. In an ancient commission for appointing beacons and watchers on the sea coast c. 1291, each watchman was to have 3d a day as a right. This regulation remained in force until the time of Elizabeth I. Before the reign of Edward III beacons tended to be little more than piles of wood sited on hilltops. At the approach of enemies the wood piles were lit. It was a haphazard affair and during Edward's reign a system of sorts was introduced and watches were kept. Each watchman was paid for a day and a night's watch. Horsemen called 'hobbelars' were stationed nearby to give notice if an enemy approached during daylight. It was 1822 before the last of these beacons was removed. Bryant's 1826 map of Norfolk shows a Telegraph Station situated on Beacon Hill.

John Loads, the village rat-catcher, lived on top of the hill in Beaconhill House. Political correctness was obviously alive and well at the 1861 census since his occupation was given as Vermin Destroyer. When I was young 'Useful' Deary lived there. Towards the end of the 19th century on a clear day it was possible to view as many as fifty parish churches from the top of Beacon Hill. When the air was crystal clear the spire of Norwich Cathedral was said to be visible. Moving westward the land between the radar station and the village drops steeply towards the cliff top. I think someone lived in an old railway carriage at The Dale many years ago. Here or here-about was the site of a tragic event in July

1951 when the charred remains of a 30 year old man from County Down were found in the embers of a large wooden hut. Three others, who were unharmed, had shared the hut. They were all labourers at the RAF camp.

Nearing the village, Sea House was built in the mid 1930s. Alexander Lang purchased the land in November 1933. The house was known originally as Bonny Rigg, and movie stars Jack Hulbert and Cicely Courtneidge stayed there, entertaining theatrical friends to parties and tennis. Journalist George Target took up residence some years later. Four Winds next door was built at much the same time as Bonny Rigg.

Considerable development was planned for this part of the village at the end of the 19th century. Poppyland was much in favour and the railway was beginning to open up the North Norfolk coast. There were ambitious plans not only for homes but for hotels and shops.

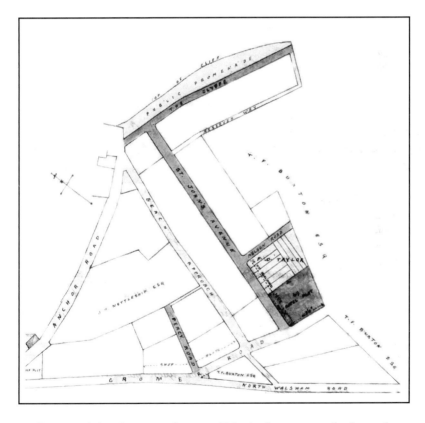

Proposed development for east Trimingham towards the end of the 19th century

The green lane between Sea House and Four Winds was to have been named St John's Avenue. Nelson Road would have led off at a right angle to the east and The Clyffe would have run parallel to the cliff top just above a public promenade. The spot upon which Sea House now stands was intended as the site for a hotel with a number of small building plots to the rear, facing Nelson Road and the sea. These plans failed to come to fruition, as did much of the development of Cliftonville in Mundesley, probably as a result of adverse publicity generated by a huge cliff fall in 1898 on the Overstrand side of Cromer.

At the far end of Beach Approach between Four Winds and Highlawns, Cliff Farm and Windy Ridge still survive on the cliff edge. The latter is believed to date from World War I. At the height of the village's popularity as a holiday resort the building was known unofficially as The Ark, from which the owners sold teas and ice creams to visitors.

Early 1900s photo of Primrose Barn (left) and Cliff Farm (centre)
The cottages seaward of Cliff Farm are long gone.

Cliff Farm and the ruins of Primrose Barn beside it are thought to date from about 1760. Over the years there have been reports occasionally of a ghostly apparition in the vicinity of Cliff Farm. The apparition takes the form of a highwayman and has, reportedly, peered in at windows and even been heard to speak on one occasion.

Cliff Farm and Windy Ridge in 2004

Highlawns looks much the same as ever, minus a hedge or two. Built in 1899, it has had a chequered past. There have been rumours of murder and suicide, with a body, again reportedly, found hanging on the 2nd floor in the early 1900s. A guesthouse run by Elizabeth Harrison in 1939, it was taken over by the Admiralty for the billeting of WRNS personnel during the 2nd World War. There is at least one underground bunker beneath the property. I played with the children living there during the late 1950s when it was once again a guesthouse. Some of the men employed in clearing the minefield stayed there from time to time.

Highlawns also served as the location for a TV drama in the 1980s. It was entitled 'Imaginary Friends' and Billie Whitelaw starred. In the grand plan for the area at the end of the 19th century the site was earmarked for shop plots. Had the plan come to fruition Highlawns would have been bisected by Percy Road. It would have provided access to land to the rear of Highlawns, held at the time by the Nettleship family from Folkestone.

Opposite Highlawns, a fork off the coast road rises in a short distance to the brow of Gimingham hill. Beyond is the steep descent into Gimingham. The road is still virtually single track, with the steep banks ground down at intervals to provide makeshift passing places. There is a fine view inland from the field at the top of the hill. We gathered nuts from the sole chestnut tree in the little copse beside the field. Gavelkind, which stood at the top of the hill until it was destroyed by fire, is believed

43

to have been owned at one time by the Jewson family. Rev. Ambrose Townsend also lived there for a while. Opposite is the track to The Beacon, apparently once bought by the Jarrold family as a holiday home but which now appears to be a smallholding. I spent a few days one summer in the early 1960s picking garlic in a field further down the hill. Midway down on the right, stands The Retreat, built in 1937/38, in part from materials reclaimed from Cliff Cottages that once stood on the cliff top behind the Crown and Anchor.

Back on the B1159, beside Highlawns and well back from the road stands Cliff House, at one time named Clyffesyde. It was inhabited by Rev. James Chadburn in 1916. At some point it served as a Convalescent Home. When I lived in Middle Street it was the home of Major Percival Pickford, D.S.O., M.C., T.D., M.A., and his wife. One of Trimingham's most notable residents, Major Pickford, was born in Plymouth and educated at Exeter School and Oxford University. He arrived in Norfolk by way of Magdalene College School, Brackley, the Oxfordshire and Buckinghamshire Light Infantry and Wellington College. He was appointed Headmaster of the Paston School in North Walsham in 1922 and remained there until he retired in 1946. A modest and likeable man, he died on January 23rd 1958.

(The only pair of cricket flannels that I ever owned belonged originally to Major Pickford. His wife offered them to me a couple of years before he died. Fortunately, despite being a bit elderly they were of excellent quality and in good condition. They even fitted rather well and served me for the entirety of what turned out to be a rather brief flirtation with cricket.)

Clyffesyde (now Cliff House), once a Convalescent Home

Beside Cliff House stand The Old Post House and Seagulls, both of which have served as the village Post Office. The Post Office has moved about Trimingham a good deal over the years. In addition to these locations it has been at The Cobbles, Charbar, The Pilgrim Shelter, The Bungalow, Bottledene, S. E. Pearson's shop and 4 Jays.

There is a cheerless empty space today between the road and the cliff top where the Crown and Anchor Hotel once stood. The earliest Licensee was Thomas Hall, a wheelwright and pump maker, who held the licence from 1845 until 1872. The hotel passed to Steward and Patteson in the early 1880s. Before the 2nd World War the Crown and Anchor and the field behind it were extremely busy with holidaymakers during the season. In the 1950s the tennis courts at the rear were popular with the Youth Club. People also travelled miles to go to the Saturday night dances.

Watney Mann took over the hotel from 1962 until September 29th 1977. By 1984 it had become a Free house. It was extensively renovated in March 1985 and then largely destroyed by fire on March 25th 1988.

HOTEL ARSON RULED OUT.
Arson has been ruled out by experts probing a big blaze at a seaside hotel. The blaze which gutted the roof of the Crown and Anchor Hotel at Trimingham near Mundesley was an accident, fire chiefs confirmed yesterday. Thirty firemen tackled the blaze. Hotel owner John Neale was quoted as saying, 'the fire was an accident, almost certainly caused by a workman who was working on the roof.' Mr Neale pledged that the hotel, which was due to reopen soon after a £70,000 facelift, would be rebuilt, 'if it is at all possible and practicable.' *EDP Saturday March 26th 1988*

Sadly, rebuilding was not possible or practicable. In January 1989 there was a proposal to convert the ruin into flats and cottages, and during the summer of 1990 it was under consideration for use as a 20-bedroom Nursing Home. Neither of these plans came to fruition and the ruin was demolished in 1992 and the site cleared.

A road known in the early 20th century as Cliff Road, (also apparently from time to time known as the Promenade or Low Lane) ran from the Crown and Anchor Hotel yard in an easterly direction towards a limekiln and the sea. In 1901 Cliff Road was in dire need of repair. At the seaward end of the road eight new houses had only recently been completed. Since more were anticipated, it seems, astonishingly, that erosion in that vicinity was considered a minimal threat at the time. It was a serious mis-calculation since not one of those buildings still stands today, and most had gone before 50 years had passed. The land that they stood on disappeared down the cliffs.

Rear view of the Crown and Anchor Hotel following the fire
of March 25th 1988

The view seaward down Cliff Road from the Crown and Anchor Hotel
The fields either side of the lane were very popular with campers.

In the proposed development plan Cliff Road was to have become Anchor Road. It gave access to the beach, Cliff Cottages and part of the cliffs once known as Trimingham Gap and later as Town House Falls. The road also provided a back entrance to Cliff House.

Towards the end of the 19th century John Bullimore and James Marshall lived at Cliff Cottages. They both worked as lime-burners at the kiln on the cliff top. In addition to burning lime James Marshall was a harness maker. He used a horse and cart to bring marl from the beach up the cliff to the kiln.

The excavation of chalk to produce lime was an ancient practice. Copious amounts of lime were used in the construction of many medieval churches and later in the brick buildings that came to replace flint and half-timbered structures.

The council received many complaints in 1897 from villagers troubled by the practice of spreading marl on the roads, since it was readily transported into people's houses. Accordingly the council decided that no marl would be spread during the summer months between the Rectory and the Crown and Anchor Hotel.

In 1891 bricklayer James Copeman lived at No 3 Cliff Cottages. I mention him since he was married to an ancestress, one Lucy Jane Kirk, daughter of John Kirk of Middle Street. Earlier, in 1881 the cottages on the cliff top were home to four brick-makers, all from Harleston. They may have worked at Mundesley where there were two brick kilns. The Mundesley Brick and Tile Company had a kiln on the west cliffs and Willaments Brickyard was located to the east. Both took clay and sand from the cliff face.

On the northern side of the Crown and Anchor Hotel was Taylor's Lane. It forked into two short tracks at the bottom of which stood more cottages on the cliff top. I remember visiting a cottage down there once, I think to attend a birthday party. Mr and Mrs J Rumsby lived down there in the early 1950s, with the barbed wire of the minefield only feet from the back yard in which their three-year-old son Roger had to play. Mrs Rumsby was reported in the paper as being terrified that the boy might get through the wire. It was only a week earlier that an exploding mine had blown in one of the windows of their cottage.

8. Water Torture

I wonder whether pump maker Thomas Hall from the Crown and Anchor made the water pump that stood for years at the roadside opposite the hotel. It was a particular irritation to father in 1946 and for the next few years that we were further than anyone else in Middle Street from the water pump. He had to carry all of our water in buckets from that pump. There were people though for whom it was worse. The family at Beaconhill House had a longer walk for their water, and it was uphill all the way home.

The village water supply was far from adequate as far back as 1898. When Col. Douglas Jones wanted to build near the Malvern Houses in Middle Street he expressed concern about the lack of water. Aware that the inhabitants of Mundesley were agitating for an improved supply he suggested that it was a good opportunity for the Parish Council to take action. It's unlikely that anything was done since the parish was still short of water over thirty years later. In 1934, the well intended to supply the new council houses at the western end of the village was dry. The clerk to the Parish Council was charged with looking into the possibility of obtaining a government grant to remedy the situation.

Nothing had changed by 1948 and the Parish Council went again to ERDC. Having got wind of a proposed new water tower close to the parish boundary for Mundesley, Trimingham asked whether they could join the Mundesley Water Scheme. There was still no hard information by March 1950. A general scheme existed to bring water from Mundesley to a water tower to be built at the Beacon. It was estimated that this would entail an increase of 2s.6d in the pound on the rates plus an extra 2s.6d for those who actually received the water.

Two years later the Parish Council learned that a water scheme was indeed under way and that Gimingham and Trimingham would be first among the rural areas to be supplied. The cost was estimated at £20,000. By late 1954 ERDC was still not in a position to name a date for completion of the water supply. Materials had been ordered but the

Girl at the foot of Middle Street beside the Pit, pre1909
Courtesy of Norfolk County Council Library and Information Service

supply route had not been finalised. By the end of the year tenders were being sought for laying the water main for Gimingham.

It emerged by June 1955 that Trimingham was to have standpipes installed except where parishioners were prepared to pay the extra cost of taking the supply to their houses. Those council houses that boasted a sink would have a single cold water tap installed. Houses without the benefit of a sink would have to use standpipes. The water supply would be extended through the village as far as the Coastguard and Bizewell Cottages on Buildings Hill in the west of the parish.

By September 1955 a water tower was nearing completion at the top of Middle Street. (It was erected on the very same piece of land that had been father's allotment in the late 1940s.) The system was finally put into operation by the end of the year.

In December 1958 the tenants of the most recently built council houses floored the council with the bizarre request that their baths be connected to the water supply. The view of ERDC was that if this were done the council house cesspools would need emptying every week. The minds of officialdom boggled at the impertinence. The ingrates would want to be connected to the sewer next!

Oh! They *were* agitating for a sewer. In March 1956 the Chairman of the Parish Council opined that the likelihood of a sewerage system in the near future was remote. He was right. More than a quarter of a century would pass. At the 1972 annual parish meeting, sewerage, along with coast protection and access to the beach were listed as the main concerns. Council house improvements were also on the agenda and in September a letter was sent to ERDC requesting new bathrooms and flush toilets. In 1973 the Parish Council sent a letter in support of Overstrand sewerage to ERDC and Norfolk County Council.

Sewerage, coastal defence, footpaths and a parish hall were the principal concerns at the annual parish meeting in 1974. The parish was told in no uncertain terms that in the sewerage stakes Mundesley, Bacton and Walcott were all considered far more important than Trimingham.

News finally came in August 1979 that a sewerage scheme was scheduled for the parish during the autumn of 1980. July that year saw a planning application for a sewage pumping station near Staden Park and a start was made on the scheme the following year. At long last the system was completed and became operational in 1982.

It is ironic that it took so long for a proper water supply and sewerage to be introduced into a village that suffered for years with the effects of too much water, albeit of the wrong type and in the wrong places. Since the beginning of time the parish has been plagued by erosion in which excessive groundwater and poor drainage have played no small part.

Flooding at the bottom of Middle Street and at the junction of the Loop Road and New Road was a persistent problem for the Parish Council. In 1910 lack of drainage at the foot of Middle Street caused the road opposite Beacon Farm to be completely flooded.

9. The Green, Middle Street and beyond

Beacon Farm stands opposite Middle Street on the B1159 or Mundesley Road. In 1839 it was the property of John Hayne, although Thomas Boardman lived in the house and actually ran the farm. When I was a child the Fairman family was in residence. The house looks much the same as it did fifty years ago although the barns and outbuildings to the rear have changed somewhat, having been converted to dwellings. There was once a pond to the east side of the farmhouse. One particularly hard winter we spent hours slithering and tumbling round the frozen pond on our bicycles in a poor simulation of ice racing.

Turning from the B1159 into Middle Street, the Green stands on the right and the remnants of a ditch or drain on the left. The drain was commonly referred to as The Pit. With flooding a perennial problem at this point The Pit was certainly in existence well over 100 years ago. We caught tadpoles and newts in its murky waters. Many times I walked home up Middle Street with wet feet, having gone into the water over the tops of my boots.

The Pit and the Methodist chapel at the foot of Middle Street

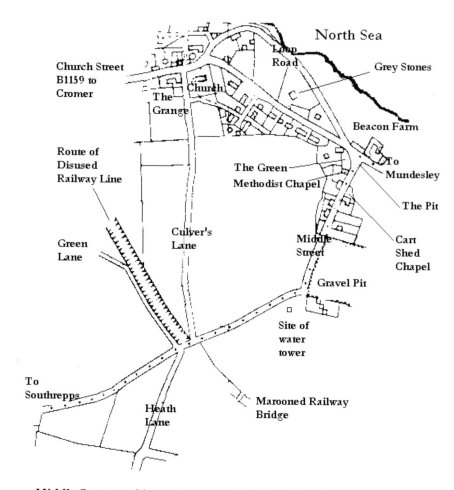

Middle Street and its environs and the Loop Road to Church Street

Reproduced by permission of the Ordnance Survey on behalf of HMSO © Crown Copyright 2007. All rights reserved. Ordnance Survey Licence number 100046946

The Green was once somewhat larger than it is today, and a footpath ran between it and the church, providing a thoroughfare between the two before the building of the New Road. Following the Coronation of Queen Elizabeth II a wooden seat was placed on The Green, one of two that were installed in the village. The other was placed on the corner opposite the church. It was rumoured at the time, apparently without foundation, that the village had been offered a choice of a playing field or two seats. Believing the rumour at the time, the youth of the village was not amused by the choice of the seats.

Numerous ideas were bandied about in early 1951, as the village sought suitable means to celebrate the Festival of Britain. H. A. Bangert suggested the planting of almond trees along New Road and an oak at the corner of Middle Street. Laudable enough but cold water was quickly poured on the proposed arboriculture. Some of those owning property on New Road objected. Permission for the oak was also thought unlikely since the erection of a bus shelter for the school children in the same location had already been turned down on the grounds that visibility for motorists would be impaired.

Mrs Seago suggested that a light be erected on The Green. Rev. R. A. Abigail countered with a proposal that the parishioners be asked to plant a profusion of flowers wherever possible and to brighten up the village generally by touching up all of their paintwork. He also felt that a village sign and a sports meeting for the children were worth consideration. Imagination obviously ran riot.

That April the parish decided to make every effort to erect a seat at the corner of New Road opposite the church, to plant bulbs in the roadside banks and flowering shrubs at the corner of Middle Street. Village signs would be erected at each end of the village, near the Crown and Anchor and at Bizewell Corner on the western boundary of the parish.

On January 26th 1953 there was a public meeting to discuss the Coronation. Somehow the Festival of Britain seats seemed to have morphed into the Coronation seats. In any event they were reported as being in position by March 1954.

A couple of cottages stand at the bottom of Middle Street beside The Green. Fishermen Tom and Theophilus (Theo) Clarke lived in one of them when I was little. The old building that was their smokehouse still stands in the back yard, covered in ivy now. On high days and holidays Tom and Theo displayed model boats on The Green. I remember seeing them about the village when I was young. Tom seemed always to wear a bowler hat and Theo was never without a sou'wester. I have the impression that I never saw them without their hats.

Near the bottom of Middle Street stands the Methodist Chapel, now converted to private residences. The chapel was built in 1909 on the site of a wood yard to replace the Primitive Methodist Cart Shed Chapel in the grounds of Three Ways further up the street. The Cart Shed Chapel was, as the name suggests, no more than a small cart or gig-shed.

In 1890 the faithful were able to attend two open air services at the Cart Shed Chapel, one at 2.30 and the other at 6.30 p.m. By 1897 only the 2.30 service survived.

THE CART-SHED CHAPEL, TRIMINGHAM.
(PRIMITIVE METHODIST CHAPEL, NTH. WALSHAM CIRCUIT.)

The foundation stone for the new chapel was laid on May 31st 1909 beneath much bunting and before a considerable crowd. In a Chapel Survey conducted in 1990 it was thought that the chapel was converted to a house in 1920. However, in 1922 the steward and Church Official was Mrs Dix and there were three services each week. By 1934 there was only one member and the circuit receipts were acknowledged to be an extremely modest 9s. 1d. I have no memory of the chapel being used for prayer although my brother thinks that it was still being used as a place of worship in the 1950s.

At that time I was attending weekly St John Ambulance First Aid classes in the chapel. Under the guidance of Billy Secker from Railway Cottages the evenings usually passed in an enjoyable and occasionally informative manner. We took turns to career back and forth on crutches or gasp menacingly from within an old gasmask. We invariably bound some unfortunate to a stretcher and tied bits of each other up with bandages. Despite the distractions most of us learned something. Later we played handball. The evenings often deteriorated into heated and largely uninformed exchanges on topics such as what to do should we encounter snow blindness or African horse sickness or if someone swallowed their tongue. If I remember correctly, the recommended course of action in the latter event seemed to entail doing something painful with a large safety pin.

Laying the Foundation stone for the new Methodist Chapel
May 31st 1909

At the top of Middle Street 'First and Last Cottage,' our old home, is still standing; although extended and much modernised. When we lived there we had no running water, electricity or sewerage. There was no kitchen or bathroom and the lavatory was a decrepit wooden lean-to. Father stole out every couple of nights or so to empty the lavatory under cover of darkness. Each tenant had a deep hole at the field edge behind the cottages, covered over with bits of board brought from the beach. No matter what time he went out to see to it father often met another shadowy figure from a neighbouring cottage engaged in the same task. In

1949 the Parish Council raised the lack of sanitation in Middle Street with the District Council. Almost a year passed before the latter responded that there was nothing that they could do. They considered the matter as one to be resolved between each landlord and tenant.

With much labour and ingenuity my parents made the cottage habitable. It was even reasonably comfortable. I have fond memories of dark winter evenings reading or drawing beside the fire that often crackled with driftwood brought from the beach. There was something rather comforting about the gentle hiss and warm glow of the Tilley lamp. The Hendry family at Church Cottage next door were good neighbours, and Uncle John, Aunt Helen and cousins David and Ian lived at 'Arter All', now Glebe Cottage, a couple of doors along.

In 2004 I was delighted when the owners kindly showed me round our old cottage. It is now an attractive and comfortable home, and a far cry from the hovel to which we moved. It is still 'First and Last Cottage,' although the name is something of a misnomer now since New Dawn Cottage has been built beyond it.

Samuel Cubitt built at least two of the cottages in the original terrace of four. On the front wall there is a stone inscribed 'S. C. 1851.' Starting out as a labourer, by 1847 Cubitt had become a farmer. At the turn of the century a number of the cottages may have been let as holiday accommodation since both Samuel and George Cubitt were offering 'apartments' for rent to holidaymakers. The Cubitts were quite a presence in Middle Street. In 1895, George from Southrepps owned the Malvern Houses, a terrace of four cottages lower down the street.

Neither father nor Uncle John was the first of the Kirk family from Gimingham to live in Middle Street, Trimingham. In 1861 a 39 year old agricultural labourer beat us all to it. An earlier John Kirk, he lived there with his wife Elizabeth, née Olley, and children George, Elizabeth and Susanna.

At the top of Middle Street there is a sand and gravel pit that has been in use since well before 1885. The annual bonfire and Guy Fawkes celebrations were held in the gravel pit during the early 1950s. We spent weeks before November 5th going door to door collecting rubbish for the fire.

In 1968 the inhabitants of the street raised a petition over traffic to and from the gravel pit and the muddy state of the road. The problem recurred in 1970 prompting discussion by the Parish Council about a letter to the police.

Beyond the gravel pit there was a sizeable garden belonging to Jimmy Storey, a resident of Middle Street who worked for Plumbley and Gaze, the coal merchants in the railway station yard. Once the site of bullock sheds, in which the owner reportedly hanged himself, Mr Storey's garden was a picture of neatness and efficiency. I went there on a few occasions for a haircut. The owner of ancient hair clippers, Jimmy could be persuaded to do the odd haircut in his shed. He certainly gave me a very odd haircut more than once. I sat on a stool in his shed doorway with an old bedspread round my shoulders and shivered in the cold while he clipped and hacked my hair into something approximating a short back and sides. Eventually I rebelled and went to Ronnie's haircutting emporium in Cromer although I am not convinced that my hair looked any better for the change.

At the top of Middle Street in the late 1940s, on the corner opposite Mr Storey's garden, there was evidence of early fly-tipping. For a while it was a good hunting ground for old, collectable glass bottles and earthenware pots. There the road turns south-west, eventually crossing the old railway bridge and heading for Blackberry Hall and Fen Farm beyond, where once lived John White who delivered milk round the village by pony and trap. After passing over the beck, which was shown in an ancient commission in 1291 to be the youthful Monesley Beck, the road eventually climbs the hill into Southrepps.

There is a veritable confluence of ways at the railway bridge, despite its being in the middle of nowhere. In addition to the main thoroughfare towards Southrepps, Heath Lane, Culver's Road and Green Lane offer other options. Heath Lane heads off left to the Brake Hill or to Grove Farm, the latter believed by some to have been the location of the far end of a smugglers' tunnel from the cliffs. Culver's Road (or Page's Lane) runs from beside Culver's Pightle down to the church and Church Street. During World War II a searchlight and gun were set up near the bridge at the end of Culver's Road. Culver's Piece stands on the south side of Green Lane.

The eastern end of Green Lane follows the line of the old railway embankment before veering off to join the road from Hall Farm to Southrepps. The lane was rerouted somewhat after the coming of the railway.

Perhaps 200 yards south-east from this bridge stands the almost identical remains of a second bridge. It is a bizarre sight now since the lane that crossed it is no more and the railway cutting that it once bridged has been filled in. As a consequence the walls of the bridge are now marooned in the middle of a field.

It must have been about 1950 when that field caught fire as grass on the embankment was ignited by sparks from a passing steam locomotive.

The fire spread up the embankment and into the field of wheat. There was great excitement that afternoon when the fire engine from Mundesley hastened up Middle Street with its bell ringing. I suppose that we were fortunate that the fire engine turned out at all. In 1905 Mundesley Parish Council invited Trimingham to subscribe one guinea per annum towards the upkeep of the fire engine. Trimingham responded that they were unable to accept the offer. Obviously someone eventually saw the light.

The dark blue brick walls of the old railway bridges survive although the deep cutting that was once beneath has long been filled in. It was in mid 1955 that it was first proposed to use the disused cutting as a rubbish dump. Despite approval from the Ministry of Health the application was at first rejected by Town and Country Planning. It was later approved and I well remember the cutting being used as a tip. It was an appalling eyesore but we spent many happy hours there, sifting through the rubbish. As with many unsupervised tips things quickly got out of hand. Fly-tipping became a problem, the wind spread rubbish far and wide and by 1969 the tip was infested with rats and had caught fire on at least one occasion. It was eventually cleared by mid 1971.

For many of the village boys it was a rite of passage to walk across the narrow walls of the bridges high above the railway line. Back when there were steam trains I watched several foolhardy souls traverse the wall enveloped in steam from a train thundering by below. I walked the walls a number of times myself but I preferred to do it without that particular distraction. Those that did it must have given one or two engine drivers a bit of a fright.

★

My parents learned in April 1950 that the council intended building two houses and two bungalows beside the Cromer Road at the western end of the village. The new houses would stand beside four existing council houses. In February 1951 the Parish Council considered ten applications for the new dwellings. Ours was one of the four names eventually selected.

10. The Loop Road and the Pilgrim Buildings

Opposite The Green is what little remains of the eastern end of the Old Coast Road or Loop Road. Once the main thoroughfare between Middle Street and Church Street it was replaced by the New Road as erosion caused the cliff edge to come ever closer. The farmer was still planting and harvesting what remained of the narrowing fields between the road and the cliff edge in the 1950s and 60s. Use of the fields came to a halt after December 1968 when a large cliff fall brought the cliff edge dangerously close to the side of the road. It was this occurrence that prompted renewed calls for coastal defences.

I remember the Loop Road with great fondness. In the company of a number of other like-minded individuals I idled away a substantial part of my childhood and early teens there, fortified with penny chews or gum from Alice Pearson's shop. The ruins of some old farm buildings next to the White Bungalow were well suited to loafing and if the wind grew a little fresh then the two walled gateways to Grey Stones afforded adequate shelter.

Originally known as Bar Haven, Grey Stones stands midway between Middle Street and the church. Once fairly isolated, it looked quite an impressive building from the road. There is little of it to be seen today, surrounded as it is by recent buildings. In the guise of Bar Haven it boasted tea-rooms and a miniature golf course and was very popular with RAF personnel from the Radar Station. Some time later an American airman and his family lived there for a short while. Heads invariably turned when they swept through the village in a huge pink, cream and chrome Pontiac.

There was an air-raid shelter in the garden of Grey Stones, built by Mr Lamb who lived there during the war. He also built a shelter at Hall Farm but it filled up with water. The air-raid shelter at Grey Stones exercised us greatly. Eventually we worked up sufficient courage to scoot across the lawn and down the mossy steps to take a look. A few old flowerpots and broken seed trays seemed poor reward for our dry mouths and thumping hearts. I worked at Grey Stones one summer holiday in the late 1950s,

The remains of the eastern end of the Loop Road.

cutting the not inconsiderable grass with an ancient and extraordinarily heavy mower.

During the early 1940s the church offered a small triangular piece of land abutting the churchyard to the Rev. A. Buxton, then the major landholder in the parish. The asking price was the princely sum of five guineas plus transfer costs. However the sale didn't proceed and the land was subsequently offered to the Road Authority for the proposed New Road between The Green and the church. Jack Bullimore from The Cobbles carried all of the hoggin for the new road with a horse and tumbrel. No one was at all surprised when the new road came to be known as the New Road.

A wartime pillbox, wire and trenches were located opposite Grey Stones beside the footpath from the church to The Green. The authorities looked at them in July 1949 but since they were considered to have no detrimental effect on local amenities they were left. In their place now stands the cul de sac Broadwood Close, so named in the early 1960s. Built on land once known as the Craft the properties were erected by Tuck for Broadwood Homes.

Certain members of the Pearson family once kept pigs on the Craft. They also used it for the training of greyhounds, the dogs chasing a rabbit skin dragged round the field behind an old car. I remember seeing Billy

Trimingham Church from the Loop Road
before the building of the New Road

Pearson riding down Church Street with a greyhound trotting on a lead beside him. I assumed that he was exercising the dog. He may well have been, but I learned recently that it wasn't unheard of for certain trainers to tire a dog in this manner prior to a race meeting at Great Yarmouth in the evening.

The village sign, designed by T. Read now stands on the corner opposite the church where once stood the second of the Coronation seats and the road foreman's heaps of sand and granite chippings. Beside the church wall the old red telephone box still stands to the left of the thatched-roof lych gate. Designed by Sir Giles Gilbert Scott, there have been few more powerful or nostalgic symbols of Britishness. The kiosk outside the church was knocked off its pedestal by a car in September 1992. Astonishingly, the telephone still worked.

Opposite the church stands The Pilgrim House, one of several properties built by Rev. Reginald C. Page, who was one of Trimingham's most distinguished characters in recent times. Born in 1872 at South Heigham, Norfolk, he was one of four brothers. Educated at Clare College and Radley Hall, Cambridge, he took his M.A. in 1897. Following an appointment in 1901 as Vicar of St John the Baptist at Whaplode Drove, Wisbech he was appointed Rector at Trimingham in 1909.

That same year there was an apportionment of income from the benefice of Methley in the diocese of Ripon, Yorks to Trimingham, Mundesley, Beeston Regis and Swafield. The parish had benefited in a similar way in 1897.

Arriving in Trimingham Rev. Page found the church in need of restoration. He threw himself enthusiastically into this work. On completion a re-opening service was held on July 19th 1911. Further restoration was funded in part by J. H. Buxton. A Sale of Work and a tennis tournament were held in the grounds of Sandy Gulls with the permission of Mr and Mrs H. A. Johnson. Major Lash ran the tennis tournament.

Rev. Page leased six acres of glebe land between the church and the cliff top from the ecclesiastical authorities. It was here that he built his bungalow, The Pilgrim House. He was later to purchase the glebe from the church authorities. Preparing to build the bungalow, he unearthed the foundations of a shelter in which he thought pilgrims may well have rested after journeying to view the head of St John the Baptist.

Within a stone's throw, beside the end of the Loop Road stands the Pilgrim Shelter, also built by Rev. Page. The Pilgrim Shelter obviously still plays an important role in parish life since a number of groups meet there. It was opened in 1935, intended as a village shelter and restroom. Rev. Page saw it as a modern replacement for the ancient shelter where pilgrims rested after their journeys. In more practical terms it was put to charitable and recreational use to improve social life in the village. In later years when the building became the Men's Club, it was upgraded with the installation of catering equipment, a billiard table and a dartboard. In 1961 Mr Philip R. Page donated the Pilgrim Shelter to the PCC. It was given over to the Parish Council upon payment of £1 in 1982.

Rev. R. C. Page outside the Pilgrim Shelter

Throughout Rev. Page's incumbency the church congregation fluctuated with the season. Numbers might have been modest through the winter but attendance swelled considerably as holidaymakers flocked to the coast through the summer. Up to 300 troops were made equally welcome during the First World War as Rev. Page acted as temporary chaplain.

Congregations of 80-100 became commonplace and in 1916 numbers touched 180. In June 1917 there was a memorial service in the church for Bernard Cubitt, who died aged 18 in a Red Cross hospital at Sittingbourne in Kent after three weeks suffering from exposure. He had been called up only three months earlier for training.

The war took Rev. Page to Brighton, Utrecht and ultimately to France where he was awarded the Overseas War Medal for his work.

As a consequence of his wife Katherine's ill health Rev. Page resigned as Rector of Trimingham to take on the temporary chaplaincy of Corfu. He hoped that the change of climate and surroundings might benefit her. They returned to England and lived for seven years at Felpham in Sussex where Rev. Page again channelled his energies into more restoration and building. They then returned to Trimingham, determined to improve the bungalow that they had left so that there would be a worthier place to be called the rectory.

Rev. Page fell foul of the Parish Council in 1933. The clerk interviewed him for sinking a large hole from which to extract sand, and for dumping rubbish close to a footpath, thereby causing an obstruction.

On the morning of March 7th 1936, aboard the *City of Nagpur* as they returned from a visit to South Africa, Mrs Page died in her sleep. She was buried at sea and a Memorial Service was held at Trimingham on April 3rd.

Still the ardent restorer and builder, Rev. Page did much to improve the church and its environs. He was a keen and talented wood-carver and several fine examples of his work are displayed on the walls of the church. In addition to the panels commemorating those who fell during the wars, a further panel depicts a scene in Corfu where Rev. Page was Acting Chaplain. The pulpit is also adorned with a carving showing Christ preaching and a prayer desk illustrates the parable of the lost sheep.

In addition to Pilgrim House and the Pilgrim Shelter he built Pilgrim Way. Now a single dwelling and a pottery, it was originally a pair of cottages constructed from the dismantled remains of a severely endangered house on the cliff edge behind the Crown and Anchor. The doomed house belonged to a Miss Pierce, for whom temporary accommodation was found in an extension to the Pilgrim Shelter. The

Pilgrim Way, built by Rev. R. C. Page

Rotunda Cottage and Bottledene, 2004

Rev. Page also built the cottages Pilgrim Rest and Pilgrim Cottage, next door to The Pilgrim House, opposite the church.

Rev. Page remarried in 1938 at the age of 66. His second wife was Lollie, widow of Rev. R. Bruce of Dehra Dun in India. Like Katherine she was interested in church work in India.

During the 2nd World War Rev. Page continued working for the church, for the soldiers billeted in the area and the social life of all. He and his wife continued living in Trimingham until his death on June 29th 1953.

Beyond the Pilgrim Shelter is what little remains of the western end of the Loop Road. White Cottage, Rotunda Cottage and Bottledene, once known as Bottle Cottage now stand perilously close to the cliff edge.

In October 1968 a Mr J. Dolan paid £4,550 for Bottledene. Some six months later he described in the *Eastern Daily Press* how he felt that the property had been rendered worthless following a huge cliff fall close to his cottage. It was estimated that 100,000 tons of material had fallen, taking a considerable chunk of the Loop Road with it.

Back in the early 1800s the cliffs below the Loop Road and the church were known as Marsh Falls. In the late 1800s one of the principal footpaths from the village to the cliff top and the beach ran from the Loop Road just to the west of Bottle Cottage.

11. 'St John, hys hede of Trymmyngham'

Since I was christened in Gimingham and my parents were not churchgoers it seems likely that my first visit to Trimingham Parish Church was in 1948 or so, to attend Sunday school. Today the parish church is in the combined benefice of Overstrand, Northrepps, Sidestrand and Trimingham. For many years it was thought to be the only church in England dedicated to the head of St John the Baptist. Mr C. E. Rawlings, our Sunday school teacher brought this intelligence to our attention. Today there are those who believe that the church is one of two so designated. Others remain convinced that Trimingham does not share the designation with any other church.

White's Directory of 1854, informs us that the church 'dedicated to St John was, in ancient times, visited by pilgrims who came with great offerings to see the head of St John the Baptist which the wily priests pretended they had got.'

It was claimed that the head was brought from the fortress of Machaerus, beyond Judea, where St John was beheaded. A number of continental abbeys made the same claim, among them Amiens and Rouen. The block upon which St John was beheaded was reputed to have been given to the church in Charing, Kent, by Richard Coeur de Lion.

William Spurdens M.A., who had seen the supposed head of St John at Amiens in the early 1800s, was of the opinion that in the case of Trimingham 'it helped the Rector without doubt, better far than his half acre of glebe, for great reverence and great offerings are made to it.' Spurdens was unable to find any relics in Trimingham but believed that, 'there was somewhere within the church a chapel of the decollation of S. John with an altar... and there doubtless the treasure was kept, and exhibited on suitable occasions.' Real or imaginary, objects of this sort certainly drew in the faithful and helped fill the coffers.

It seems unlikely that there was ever any true basis for the Trimingham claim since the church has not endured as a place of note for pilgrimage. Probably the head was one of a number of those representing the Baptist that were manufactured in Burton-on-Trent and Nottingham

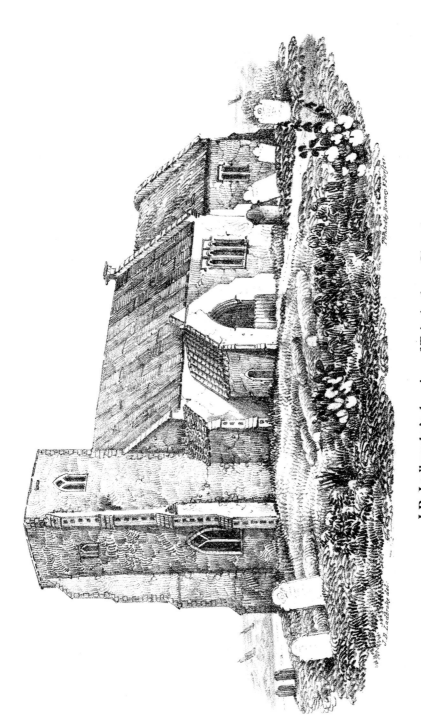

**J.B. Ladbrooke's drawing of Trimingham Church
with thatched roof, pre-1879.**
Courtesy of Norfolk County Council Library & Information Service

from alabaster from Chellaston, Derbyshire, in the 15th century. Certainly a number were set up in churches as objects of devotion.

The church itself is built of flint with stone dressings, mainly in the Perpendicular style with some earlier work incorporated. It consists of a chancel, a nave with a south porch and a low western tower dating from about 1300 and believed to be unfinished. The font dates from the early 14th century.

Trimingham Church

During the reign of Henry VII (1485-1509) the church received a magnificent rood screen, which today separates the chancel from the nave and has on each side of a central arch two bays, open in the upper portions and adorned below with painted panels of saints, kings and martyrs.

The identity of some of those depicted has been disputed. (Alternatives suggested by various authorities are shown below in italics.) The *Norwich Mercury* reported at the end of the 19th century that from the south side the figures were as follows:-

S. Petronilla, the reputed daughter of S. Peter, a virgin with turban, book in her right hand and key in left. (The sign of the Lamb and Flag can be seen in the spandrel.)

S. Cecilia, virgin, book in left hand and sprig of red flowers in other. (Martyr, the patron of church music. A dragon can be found in the spandrel.) *[St Dorothy]*

S. Barbara, palm branch in right hand and castle *[portable organ]* in other. (Martyr, holding a pen and an axe.) *[St Cecilia]*

S. Edward, K.M., male figure in turban, long hair, short beard, wearing armour, only feet and hand, rest covered by two garments; hawk and lure in right hand. *[St Jeron]*

On the north side:-

S. Edmund, crowned, arrow and sceptre, green robe and ermine tippet. (King and martyr, who like St Sebastian was shot to death with arrows. He carries an arrow in his right hand and a sceptre in his left.)

S. Clare, abbess, friend and follower of S. Francis of Assisi, nun, with book in left and remonstrance in right hand.

S. Clement, P.M., a Bishop, with double cross staff in left hand, right raised, wears green cope, red dalmatic and alb, in benediction, anchor at foot. *[St James the Greater]*

S. John Baptist, long flowing hair, feet naked. In the spandrel is S. John's head on a charger. *[James the Great] [St Felix]*

The screen was lost for many years, presumably removed during the Reformation. It was discovered by Archdeacon Cross in a farm barn around 1865. In 1891 part of the screen, which was then replaced in the church by a replica in modern oak, was included in a collection given or bequeathed by Bartholomew William Spaull to Norwich Castle Museum. Spaull was a builder and carver and clerk of works at Norwich Cathedral. When reclaimed by Trimingham the screen was restored to its rightful position. In 1900 T. Hugh Bryant found the screen 'in good preservation.' A century on, it bears evidence of abuse and worm infestation.

The Communion cup or chalice was described in the PCC Minute Book in 1946 as 'One silver cup, weighing about 7 oz Troy, with inscription 'Trimyngham Anno 1568,' made by Peter Peterson of Norwich in 1567.' It was presented to the church the following year. The chalice is rather fragile now. It is used only on special occasions; the last time being in June 2002 for the Queen's Golden Jubilee and the dedication of a new gravestone to mark the burial place of the crew of a Dutch vessel, *De Vrouw Arendje*.

In 1552 the church had three bells. In 1746 Churchwarden Robert Plumbley sold two bells, one being cracked and the other not hung. The proceeds were used for repairs since the church was said to be falling down. In 1900 there was only one bell, the sole survivor of a set of four. It was inscribed '+ Ric's Baxter, Brazier de Norwyco fecit me.'

In 1939 Messrs Mears & Hainbanks of Whitechapel repaired the church bell at a cost of £57.12s.0d. The bell frame was strengthened and the bell re-hung with completely new fittings. It was rung up and found to be in good order. It was noted that the bell would not need re-greasing until 1949 at the earliest. The same year a new portion of churchyard to

The organ in Trimingham Church, made in 1888, thought to be the only surviving instrument by John Windus of London

the east of the church was formed from an ancient archery ground. For many years this land had been combined wrongfully with adjoining landholdings. Being glebe land it was recovered for the church during the incumbency of Rev. A. G. Townsend.

In 1951 the PCC received the offer from Rev. R. C. Page of a gift of six new bells. The chiming bells were to be purchased from Whitechapel Bell Foundry. Loughborough Bell Foundry advised that the church tower was not strong enough to support six ringing bells. In fact it was an oak beam that was insufficiently strong.

Hanging near the font is a watercolour painting of the church during the course of restoration. Painted by Sir Alfred East, the painting was exhibited in Buenos Aires as an example of English art. It was presented to the church by a friend of Rev. R. C. Page following the artist's death.

The church was restored in 1820 when the floors were tiled and again in 1859. Several memorials and brasses were obscured, including a brass in the chancel for William Paston, one of the sons of Sir William Paston. The brass had not been obscured in 1851.

Spurdens visited the church on June 1st 1822 and declared 'the church is without aisles, and has a clumsy low square tower.' He also spotted the final resting place of 'the body of Mr Robert Bidbanck, sometime preacher of the gospel in this town who died the 15th...of April...' Spurdens supposed him to be 'the intrusive Puritan minister, during the Commonwealth, which may account for his name not appearing in Blomefield's List of Rectors.

In 1859 the Rector, the Rev. A. B. Cross raised £1500 by subscription for further restoration. Open bench seats for 200 souls were erected at the same time. The organ was built by John Windus of London for St John's Church, Trimingham in 1888. The only known organ by this builder, it was restored in 1972 by Storr's of Neatishead in memory of R. C. Page, Katherine and Constance Page.

In 1892 the Rector William Tatlock added a vestry on the north side of the chancel. At this time the church collections were used for a number of good causes, prominent among them the London Jews' Society and Cromer Cottage Hospital.

There is a handwritten note inside the back cover of the Churchwarden's Accounts 1894-1903. 'Miss Trimingham, 65 Hungerford Road, London N and of Caldecot Towers, Bushey Heath, Herts - whose ancestors 500 years since were Lords of this parish.'

Rev. R.C. Page discovered much about the church and parish, tracing Rectors back to the first recorded incumbent, William de Rollesby in 1294.

Rectors of Trimingham

Date

1294   William de Rollesby

1316   Nicholas de Castleacre

1317   Richard Pykot, with Poryngland, - by John, Earl Warren

1324   William de Haya, of Runton, - ditto

1349   James de Platea - by Henry, Earl of Lancaster

1384   William de Pountfrevit, - by John, King of Castile, etc.

1392   William de Bynnebrook, - ditto

1393   John Salteby, *alias* Lanun, with Swaby Linc, - ditto

1405   Robert Tymworth, with Martham, - by the King

1411   William Stoke, with Chesterton, Ely - ditto

1419   Richard Proo, with S. Clement ad Pont, Norwich, - ditto

1424   William Pete, with Ketleburgh, - by Archbishop of Canterbury feoffee of Henry V

1434   John Grimesby, - ditto

14--   John Hore

1448   William Powel, - by the King

1457   Thomas Eyre, - ditto

1464   John Stery

1471   Richard Colfox, - by the Queen

1477   William Stokes, - ditto

There are obviously some incumbents missing at this point.

1603   James Matchett, - by the Queen, returned 67 Communicants.

1637   William Noyes M.A. – by the King

16--   Thomas Cooke

----   John Mountford, ob. 1721.

1721   Edward Bilston, ob. 1756, - by the King

1756   William Clagget, - ditto

1775   Stephen Gage, - by Duchy of Lancaster

1816   Robert Steele, ob.1857, - ditto

1828   A. B. Cross, - ditto

1860   E. Foster Hutton, - ditto

1861   William Aubrey Cutting, - ditto

1867   Charles Chapman McArthur, - ditto

1873   Abraham Matchett, - ditto

1883   Thomas Romaine Govett, - ditto

1886   William Tatlock, M. A.

1900   Alfred O. Smith, - by exchange

1909   Reginald C. Page

1923   A. G. Townsend

1941   D. G. Townsend
1946   Arthur H. Harper, B. A.
1949   Robert A. Abigail, M. A.
1959   W. T. Taylor.
1965   Charles H. Shells, M. A. - 1st Rector of the Trunch Group of Parishes which included Trimingham
1971   Garth Norman, M. A.
1985   John Randall, M. A.
1995   Simon Habgood, B. Th. - 1st Rector of Combined Benefice of Overstrand, Northrepps, Sidestrand and Trimingham.
1999   Michael L. Langan, B. A.

*

In 1944 it was agreed that the church cleaner and a woman helper would each receive 15/- for cleaning the church floors and pews; 5/- extra would be paid to the woman who cleaned beneath the heating pipes under the metal gratings in the church floor. A few years later there were certain elements of the Sunday school class who routinely took up the gratings every Sunday morning to see whether any collection money had fallen through and lodged beneath those heating pipes.

For several years up to 1958 there were few or no confirmation candidates in the parish. It was the view of the Rector, Rev. R. A. Abigail, that 'the young people of the village were not receiving from their elders the spiritual interest and encouragement to which they were entitled.' He described us as 'in very truth, deprived children.' I recall Rev. Abigail inviting several of us down to The Rectory at Gimingham for tea one afternoon. I was surprised that he barely mentioned the church, intent instead on trying to persuade us to attend the Whist Drives that were held in Trimingham School hall at the time. I can't imagine why he thought we would be interested.

When the major landholder, Rev. Arthur Buxton, died, he left £200 to the church. Rev. Abigail suggested that the parish take the opportunity to buy the old school for use as a Village Hall. A village meeting was called to discuss the future of the school but in a response typical of the time only nine people attended. The school was eventually sold in 1963 and converted to a private residence. This was a poor outcome so far as the village was concerned, but entirely predictable in view of the apathetic response to the village meeting.

12. Church Farm, Church Street and a Shopkeeper Extraordinaire.

Pushing through brambles on the piece of ground behind the church in 2004 I was astonished to see that 'Faraway' was still standing. An old construction of timber and asbestos sheets it was once the property of a man by the name of Rump. In November 1945 there was something of a contretemps between him and ERDC concerning the Right of Way between Middle Street and the back of the church. The records are silent on the outcome. In addition to 'Faraway', Mr Rump kept a caravan on the cliff top. He was often seen about the village accompanied by a Sealyham terrier. Revisiting the site in 2007 I discovered that 'Faraway' was indeed far away, the decaying ruin having been demolished to make way for a new building.

'Faraway', 2004

Beside the church, The Grange looks much as I remember it. The garden has been extended to take in a small meadow where we celebrated the Coronation of Queen Elizabeth II with a fête after parading round the village in fancy dress. The old barns and outhouses of Church Farm have been converted into residences, Manor Barn, Church Barn and St John's Barn. I played in those barns when they housed little more than worm-infested tumbrels, seed-drills and the like. Pitchforks, thatching tools and a scythe hung on the wall and in a corner stood a device for chopping cattle cake. The smell of rodent and rotting root crops was pungent in the air.

The Grange

John Warnes, a landowner and gentleman of independent means, his wife Louisa and their children, lived at The Grange in the mid 19th century. They employed six servants. Warnes was indefatigable in promoting the cultivation of flax, a plant first introduced by the Romans. Only 400-500 acres of flax were grown in Norfolk in 1843. In 1844 Warnes published a pamphlet entitled 'Extracts from Ancient and Modern Writers on the Flax Crop - selected and arranged by John Warnes Jun. Esq. Trimingham, Norfolk.'

Warnes was keen to remove the prejudices against the cultivation of the flax plant. The intolerance and antipathy prevalent at the time were founded on the erroneous impression that flax was more exhausting to the soil than any other crop. Warnes and other like-minded individuals swore that the opposite was the case. 'A better crop of wheat was never seen on the land than that which succeeded my flax.' He was instrumental in setting up the National Flax and Agricultural Improvement Society, of which a branch was formed on January 18th 1844 at Fakenham. Thomas Brown at Hall Farm was also a flax enthusiast.

Robert Beckett owned and lived at Church Farm towards the end of the century. It was generally known as Page's farm when I was a child, Robert Page being the farmer and sons Norman and Claud being much in evidence. It was eventually taken over by Godfrey Thornton and his family.

Our old Sunday school teacher Mr Rawlings and his wife lived in Pilgrim Rest opposite the church. For several years he invited one or two of us that didn't have access to a TV round to his house to watch the F. A. Cup Final. At half time he slipped along to Alice Pearson's shop to return with a block of ice cream, sometimes vanilla, occasionally Neapolitan, which we ate with antique tea-spoons from cut glass bowls. For a time a TV newsreader and his family lived at Pilgrim Cottage next door. I did a little part-time gardening for them one holiday when I was 14 or 15. By the end of that summer I was convinced that I was deeply in love with the newsreader's wife despite the fact that she was married, had a baby, must have been almost twice my age and had given me no encouragement whatever.

Next door to the Pilgrim cottages was Alice Pearson's shop. Other shops had come and gone. Benjamin Rust of Cromer bought property in Trimingham in 1813 and kept a shop in the village until 1922 or thereabouts. Henry Pycraft also had a shop in the village in 1838. By the time I took any interest in shopping Alice Pearson was the sole shopkeeper in the village. Sadly, her shop at the top of Church Street is no more. 'S. E. Pearson, Grocer and General Stores,' was named after her mother, Sarah Ellen Pearson who opened up in about 1926. Before my time there were tea rooms in the cottage next door to the shop. I believe they closed in about 1940.

During the 1950s and 60s a visit to Alice's emporium was never less than interesting. Normally something of a glorious muddle, the shop could be a source of surprises, the scene of occasional triumphs and inevitably the odd disappointment. If one wasn't pushed for time a visit could even be entertaining.

Ding, ding, ding, ding, ding. The bell on the shop door seemed as though it might ring for ever sometimes.

'Hello, Alice. Have you any gravy browning?'

'Ah. Now, let me see. I'm sure I've got some somewhere. That only came in... Now where did I put that? I know I saw some, only yesterday, I think. When Mrs what's-her-name came in. Or was it Mrs..? You know...'

Pearson's tea rooms and shop in Church Street, about 1940

Alice's voice tailed off uncertainly and she would lift up one or two things close at hand, a look of puzzlement on her face. A newsagent, grocer, greengrocer, confectioner and tobacconist, theoretically Alice could meet almost any requirement. If she could actually put her hand upon it one could buy just about anything. A bootlace or a reel of thread, a comb or an ounce of Juggler Mild, a postcard of Trimingham, only slightly creased, a crumpled magazine or a packet of Grape Nuts. If she couldn't locate what one wanted, always willing and ever helpful, Alice often came up with an imaginative alternative... and then spent an age trying to find it.

I was in the shop once, behind a woman seeking a tin of peaches for her husband's Saturday lunch. Alice couldn't locate one but offered instead a can, contents unknown since the label was missing. 'I'm nearly sure they're peaches,' she said. 'That's the right size. And that's only got a little dent. Do you want to take it?' On my way home I met the purchaser heading back grim-faced to the shop. 'Look at this,' she said, producing from beneath the front of her coat a jagged-topped tin of carrots.

We were forever on the lookout for empty Corona bottles to take back to the shop since Alice paid a few pence for the empties. We couldn't believe our luck when we stumbled across a cache of soda siphons in the bramble bushes behind the old school lavatories. The siphons were green with algae but, after they had been given a bit of a wash in the rain water butt, to our astonishment Alice paid something like 1s. 3d each for them.

Today there is no sign that the cottage was ever a shop. Gone are the crumbling *papier-mâché* bananas that hung in the window. Away are the chewing gum machine and the newspaper racks from the wall. Buried in the churchyard in 1985, alongside her parents William and Sarah Ellen, Alice Pearson was once a shopkeeper without equal.

★

Church Street is still as narrow as ever and without the benefit of footpaths or street lighting. Both are issues that have been debated in the parish for decades. In 1934 Church Street was made up and 'an apology for a path' created. The villagers were outraged since they considered the street even more dangerous than it had been before the work was done. Four years later they sought a 30-mph speed limit from the council houses at the west end of the village up to Highlawns in the east.

In 1946 some optimistic soul approached the council requesting street lighting. The chairman undertook to contact the Electric Light Co. After years of intermittent debate, in 1963 the council decided not to go ahead with street lighting. However a year later, after receiving a letter on the cost of providing street lighting from the Eastern Electricity Board they called a public meeting. Not a single member of the public attended and the apparent lack of interest led to no further action being taken.

Questions of footpaths and street lighting surfaced again in 1969. The inescapable fact was that the main road was simply not wide enough for a footpath. At a parish meeting in 1970 a number of issues were raised, among them street lighting, again. Preservation of Beacon Hill as an open space, and the provision of yet more public seats also appeared on the agenda. The proposal for street lighting was defeated by 5 to 1 six months later. Again, no further action was taken.

Upper Church Street

I have often wondered at the extraordinary level of apathy that has been a feature of the village from time to time. The *Norfolk Chronicle* made reference to it on December 20th 1918.

'There was not a great amount of activity on Saturday at the Mundesley polling station which included the electorate from the villages of Knapton, Trunch, Gimingham and Trimingham. Out of a possible 1089 on the register, only 601 went to the poll. A newly enfranchised lady voter was an early comer, the majority voting before the noon hour. An elector with no arms and seven or eight illiterates were amongst those who visited the poll. Occasionally one came across a voluble elector, who announced with no uncertain sound, his intention to vote for Lloyd George, the war winner, whilst from others not a gleam could be gathered which of the two candidates were in the most favour. A prophet would indeed be bold to forecast the state of the political barometer in this, the southern extremity of the North Norfolk constituency. Apathy reigned on both sides to a certain extent, but now and again there were some illuminating sidelights.'

The article makes a fair enough point, although the tone is to a degree patronising and illustrative of the way in which Trimingham and certain other small, rural seaside villages were viewed.

When I was a child I heard adults in the village opine on numerous occasions that there was little or no point in trying to change anything. It was a cry soon learned by some of their children. To raise an objection, attend a meeting, or perhaps write a letter, even to vote, was believed by many to be futile because 'they'll just go ahead and do whatever they want to do regardless, like they always do.' 'They' were the government, the council, the landowners, the farmers and perhaps the better educated and certain in-comers who were sufficiently motivated to seek change. There are those that still propound the view today.

Mere mention of the Parish or District Council was likely to be greeted with a groan, a knowing look, a hoot of derision or rolling of the eyes. Many of the locals obviously felt less than empowered.

At the time the Buxton family were the major landholders. The bulk of the remainder of the land was in the hands of a few farmers. The majority of the population rented rather than owned their dwellings, and a number lived in houses or cottages owned by their employer.

Back in the late 1940s and 50s I suspect that the apparent lack of interest that frequently prevailed in local matters was to a degree the response of people wearied by the war, many disoriented and now finding themselves with families to support and with little money and few possessions. Many lived in accommodation of inferior quality and without the benefit of the most basic services. In addition they or their parents had seen the council and the landowners 'do whatever they want to do, regardless,' on numerous occasions.

Roughly 90% of the male working population in the parish in the early 1950s was employed in labouring or other unskilled or semi-skilled work. The men worked long hours as farm or builders' labourers, painters and decorators or fishermen. Others delivered coal, milk, bread or post or worked on the railways or the buses. Of the remaining 10% or so of the adult male population, roughly half were retired and the other half were farmers, landowners, schoolteachers or in business. Several of the women worked too, a number of them out in the fields as fruit and vegetable pickers. Wages were often less than generous and many families had to scrimp and save to make ends meet.

For the majority, some aspects of life were less than straightforward or convenient. Going to work or school might be on foot, by bicycle or by bus. Some journeys required a train onward from Mundesley or Cromer. The return meant the same again, with the traveller often arriving home late. Quite apart from the day's labour, water had to be fetched from the pump or the well, wood had to be gathered, sawn and chopped, hens fed, gardening done and the lavatory emptied. If there was any time after that, several men fished, hunted rabbits or kept an allotment to supplement the family diet. For the women, after the children had gone to school, on washing day the copper had to be filled and lit, shopping done and meals prepared. Cooking was done on the range or over an open fire. When it was wet the washing that had taken most of the day would still not be dry and it was festooned about the already crowded living accommodation. On other days there was baking, ironing, mending and a myriad other activities including shopping that entailed a bus or train journey to Cromer, Mundesley or Norwich. Such a trip could take the entire day.

For many, merely trying to keep body and soul together left little time for much else. There was the public bar at the Crown and Anchor Hotel or the Men's Club but they weren't to everyone's taste, and not everyone had money to spend on beer. There was no playing field and there were no sports teams other than those hastily put together on an ad hoc basis. For many there was little to do in the village. As a consequence village spirit, belief or esteem was low or virtually non-existent. And if that was not enough, the people of Trimingham had to sit back and watch their neighbouring villages grow and prosper. They, of course, enjoyed the services and amenities that Trimingham lacked, and they had the use of their beaches.

Perhaps it's not so difficult to see how such a people might be a touch apathetic.

In Church Street Grange Cottage was the site of William Warnes' smithy in 1901. When I was a child it was home to Claud and Maud Page. I had to climb up a ladder and through an upstairs window once when Maud locked herself out.

On the other side of the road stand several flint cottages, built in the 1800s in what was previously a stack yard. Fisherman and builder Tom Kidd lived at No. 16 and fish merchant George Clarke lived next door; George had a smokehouse in his yard. He collected fish from the afternoon train and delivered round the village, sometimes by means of a cart on bicycle wheels, sometimes by motorcycle and sidecar or in an Austin van. He was believed by some to wish away warts.

Beyond The Cobbles and School House stands Buxton Hall, originally the school but a private residence for years now. The school was built in 1849 by the Buxton family for the education of poor children, and they continued to support it for some time. The landlord, John Henry Buxton, made an agreement on April 28th 1903 with the tenant, Rev. Alfred Owen Smith. It provided for rental of the school at 1s. per year and rental of the school house at £10 per year. The Foundation Managers for the school were A. O. Smith, Henry Fowell Buxton, Robert Beckett and George Cubitt.

In 1917 there were 47 pupils. Attendance was endlessly problematic. The teachers did their best against an unremitting stream of absences through influenza, coughs and colds, whooping cough, mumps and other ailments. The records show that an alarming number of children suffered broken bones, debilitating sprains or gashes. Heavy snow and rain also took its toll. Sometimes in the depths of winter there were no fires because coal was unobtainable.

Despite the difficulties, the school was well run. It was also well scrutinised. School inspectors, the nurse, the dentist, the needlework inspectress, the drill instructor, the Rector and members of the Buxton family all visited regularly. After one of his annual inspections the Rector expressed serious concern about one of the pupils who had failed his examination. Rev. Page noted in the school records that the boy in question seemed particularly slow and had great difficulty learning. He wondered what on earth would become of the child. By delightful irony that boy became the man who eventually bought the school.

By 1930 the roll had shrunk to 26. There was a limit to what the school could offer. Occasional gardening for the older boys and a small flower garden for the younger children offered a little relief from book work. Girls received no domestic instruction beyond needlework. Numbers dropped again in 1932 and the school closed for educational purposes on April 30th that year, for reasons of national economy. Owned at the time by Rev. Arthur Buxton, it was left to the village for use as a village hall. In future the children would be taken by charabanc to the Belfry School in Overstrand.

Church Street - the School is on the right

In 1939 Rev. Buxton expressed great disappointment at the misuse of the school buildings. There had been drinking in the yard. Undesirables from other places frequented it, and the playground was in a deplorable condition. He considered closing the premises altogether.

From the late 1940s we attended village functions there. The old school was the venue for children's Christmas Parties, magic lantern shows, jumble sales, dances, whist and beetle drives. We even enjoyed the odd visiting conjurer and the occasional revue and play. From time to time the youth club was resurrected and met there.

Hall Farmhouse is listed as a building of Special Architectural or Historic interest. It was probably built in the 17th century and remodelled in the late 18th century. When I was a child the entrance to the farmyard at Hall Farm was opposite the gateway to the railway station yard. Between the two was a small triangle of grass. We ruined numerous bicycle tyres, wheels and the soles of our plimsolls racing round the

Hall Farm

The Rectory in 1912

triangle and performing extravagant broadsides on the sloping gravel entrance to the farm.

Just inside the farm gate there was a pond, said to be so deep that it would cover a carthorse's back. We never knew whether we believed that story or not, but it kept us from venturing onto the pond when it froze over. We had little need to brave the pond since just below the railway bank at the far end of the station yard was Page's pit. Each winter it became a wide but comfortingly shallow expanse of water. Whenever it froze to a sufficient thickness we could play on it with impunity.

Opposite Hall Farm stands the Old Rectory. In the outhouses on the corner of the Southrepps Road and the Cromer Road there was once a tiny cloakroom and a lavatory behind a roadside door let into the cobbled wall. We used it for years as a shelter as we waited for the school coach to Overstrand or the Eastern Counties buses to Mundesley or Cromer. The shelter was a godsend throughout the winter so long as one didn't lean against the whitewashed walls in one's school blazer.

Christmas Party in the old School building in the 1950s

13. Working the Land

During the 18th century the families of Clipperton, Plumbley and Nurse farmed much of Trimingham. By the early 19th century the main landowners were Thomas Nurse, Joseph Newman, Stephen Gilham and Edward Lyttleton, Bart. In 1829 John Warnes at The Grange and William Bacon were the major landholders. Hannah Rust lived at the Old Rectory and held land in the vicinity of what is now Staden Park.

The 1838 Parish Map of Trimingham by George Playford (Land Surveyor) showed the parish to be 523 acres. Francis Bacon had taken over Hall Farm and the major portion of the land. The farm was occupied by Thomas Brown. Other significant parcels of land in the parish were owned by John Warnes, Edward Long, John Hayne and Richard Newman. Long was the owner of Bizewell Farm where Priest Green was the occupant. At the eastern end of the village the land east of Cliff Farm belonged to Stephen Gilham and was farmed by Benjamin Payne. Richard Newman owned the Old Rectory. John Wortley held land at Clapham Dams where James Emery was the occupant. At this time Thomas Fowell Buxton, Samuel Hoare and Lord Suffield each owned only a small portion of land in the parish.

Sir E. N. Buxton and Lord Suffield had become the main landowners in Trimingham by 1845. Suffield was the Lord of the Manor. In addition to Trimingham the Buxton family held estates in a number of neighbouring parishes. They continued to hold the major portion of land in Trimingham for the next 120 years or so.

Census returns in the mid 19th century indicate that there were eight or nine farmers in the parish, between them employing more than 22 agricultural labourers. George Wright farmed 190 acres and employed seven men and two boys; Stephen Gilham held 120 acres. More modestly John Fox and Daniel Long worked nine acres each.

Towards the end of the century much of the farmland in the parish had been consolidated among fewer farmers. Abraham Wright farmed 240 acres; Robert Beckett at the Grange farmed 230 acres and employed ten labourers. Samuel Bates worked 95 acres.

Apart from a few brief intervals agriculture was in depression from the middle of the 19th century until the 2nd World War. Land under cultivation was reduced by 20% in the 30 years prior to 1901. This was due in large measure to the low prices of imports from the Americas and the colonies. The 1st World War improved the position of the industry but it was a short-lived boom. Men returning to 'a land fit for heroes,' found themselves jobless or forced to suffer ruinous wage cuts. The Norfolk farm worker and his family suffered.

In 1923 farm workers came out on strike. They returned to work with wages set at 25s. per 50-hour week and overtime of 6d per hour. With the payment of subsidies to farmers and with higher wages and paid holidays for the farm workers, conditions on the farms gradually improved. In Trimingham, as elsewhere, there were those who left and sought work in other places.

During the 2nd World War the government gave priority to food production and agriculture benefited greatly. Produce from the Buxton estates was sold in a shop named the Trimingham Dairy at 5 Church Street, Cromer until 1946.

There followed the post-war years of agricultural prosperity. However it was accompanied by increasing mechanisation and the subsequent loss of the vast majority of farm workers' jobs. As the farm labourers moved out, retired or died, the composition of rural villages began to change. Commuters and retired people moved in.

The Harrison family came to Trimingham in about 1890. They came from West Norfolk and settled at Clapham Dams Farm on the outskirts of the parish. Albert Harrison remained there but Chris Harrison and his family moved to Hall Farm. A pleasant man, Chris was instantly recognisable. Rarely seen without his pipe, his stick and his dog, we often saw him as he stumped about the village in a worn hat and wellington boots. Reliant on true horsepower, he farmed in rather a different way from that practised today. Significant amounts of hay and oats were grown for feed in those days, as well as sugar beet, wheat and barley for malting. He kept cattle until 1947, when he finally disposed of his last 27 beasts.

The other farmers at that time were Fairman at Beacon Farm, Brown Gotts, who had land in the east of the parish, Godfrey Thornton who took over from the Page family at Church Farm, and Alfred Hicks at Bizewell Farm.

Today virtually all of the farmland in Trimingham is owned by E. G. Harrison & Co. They grow sugar beet, wheat, barley and a few peas, but by far their greatest interest is in potatoes. They currently produce in the region of 15,000 tons of potatoes per annum for the crisp market.

During the 1950s the principal landowner, Rev. Arthur Buxton held a shoot each autumn in the woods planted in the mid 1800s by Thomas Fowell Buxton. I went beating on one such occasion when the gamekeeper had been let down. We drove through Hulver Hill, Flowers' Plantation and Runny Hill, then on to the railway embankment, Young Plantation and Long's Hill.

Three things stuck in my mind about that day. One of the guns, a youngish fellow, looking slightly foolish in an over-large cap and knickerbockers, was sent home mid-morning. Somewhat ill-advisedly, he had taken a shot from out in a field towards a line of beaters on the railway embankment. I was one of those beaters. Some old fellow well behind me took some lead shot in a little finger. Fortunately that was the extent of the damage. Otherwise Godfrey Thornton from The Grange lived up to his reputation as a crack shot by bringing down a multitude of birds including several woodcock. The other guns had a good day, including a very satisfactory lunch at the Shooting Lodge near the edge of Long's Hill Wood.

The Lodge was a timber building on dwarf brick walls, surrounded by woods and rhododendron walks and with a fine view out to the coast. We beaters helped ourselves to a selection of cold meats, cheese and pickles in an adjoining shed. Although I was only 14 or so I was invited to help myself to a couple of bottles of beer. The afternoon passed most pleasantly as we sallied out to the Rome Plantation. At the end of the day I wobbled home along Buck's Heath Lane on my bike with 30 shillings in my pocket and as many rabbits and pigeons as I could carry.

Comparing the landscape today with that which existed when I was a child it is striking just how many trees, hedges and banks have disappeared, presumably in the pursuit of agricultural excellence.

Buck's Heath Lane in 1910

14. The Coming and Going of the Railway, the Station and its environs.

The railways played a significant role in opening up parts of the North Norfolk coast. However East Anglia was not in the vanguard so far as rail was concerned. The service arrived late and slowly.

The East Norfolk Railway completed a service from Norwich to North Walsham in 1874. An extension to Cromer opened in March 1877, connecting the resort with the Great Eastern mainline to Liverpool Street in London.

By 1883 there was an excellent service between Norwich and Cromer. Seven trains ran each day. In June 1887 the Eastern and Midlands Railway arrived at the new Cromer Beach station, giving access from London King's Cross. By the end of the century a journey from Liverpool Street to Cromer took 2 hours 55 minutes and cost 10s. for a weekend return.

The Midland & Great Northern railway was formed as a joint venture to open up the hitherto relatively inaccessible stretch of coast between Cromer and Happisburgh. The newly formed Norfolk and Suffolk Joint Railways Company began a service to Mundesley on July 1st 1898. They hoped to transform Mundesley into a major resort. The railway certainly stimulated some development but the Company overbuilt Mundesley station, installing three platforms, each 600 feet in length. The opening service was optimistic in the extreme with 16 trains running daily. It was reduced the following year. Plans for a branch line to Happisburgh were advanced but came to an abrupt halt about 1907.

Until 1898 the Joint Railways Company was planning a route from Mundesley to Cromer that would take the track well to seaward of both Bizewell Farm and Sidestrand Church. They must have reconsidered a route so close to the cliff edge in view of the huge cliff fall that took place between Cromer and Overstrand during that year. On November 29th 1898 at 11.00 a.m. they deposited a plan for a proposed deviation of the route, taking the track inland from the vicinity of Bizewell Farm to a point close to the Jermy's Mill House in Sidestrand. The total length of the deviation was 2 miles, 3 furlongs, 0.7 chains.

The Mundesley to Cromer service, by way of Trimingham and Overstrand, opened on August 3rd 1906. The *Eastern Daily Press* reported the event the following day.

> Our Mundesley correspondent writes he was on Mundesley railway station at 6. 45 a.m. on Friday morning and secured the first return ticket to Cromer Beach Station. The station master was early in attendance, and on the alert to see that everything was in order. The train left punctually at the registered time, 7.15; reaching Trimingham at 7.22, Overstrand 7.30, and Cromer 7.40. The journey out and back was a very delightful one, the whole distance constantly presenting charming views of inland scenery on one side and the expanses of the German Ocean on the other. The companies concerned have spared no pains nor expense in making the new piece of coast line as perfect as possible. The rails are laid very even and regular, and there is little or no oscillation, and the signal boxes with their various machinery are quite up-to-date. There will be a good service of trains by the GE Company, and also the Midland and Great Northern Joint during the next two months, and doubtless the new line will be very largely patronised by residents and visitors.

An excited crowd gathered at Trimingham station to witness the arrival of the first train. The station opened with a Station Master, two signalmen, two porters and a clerk. The Company built the line at a cost of £93,000. A London to Sheringham through service began in July 1906 and the Norfolk Coast Express first ran in the summer of 1907, non-stop from Liverpool Street to North Walsham. At North Walsham three coaches were detached for Sheringham and two for Overstrand, via Mundesley and Trimingham. The main portion of the train ran into Cromer High station.

Never as successful as anticipated, the Norfolk Coast Express service ended in 1914. The service from Mundesley to Cromer never flourished in the way that had been envisaged; it lost money in its first year and made a modest profit in the second. The railway brought plenty of holidaymakers but little growth to Trimingham. It was a great disappointment to the railway companies who had collaborated to provide an efficient service.

Mundesley was not the only example of over-building. The railways overbuilt along the coast generally. Access to Trimingham station was by means of wooden steps down to the platform from the Southrepps Road

Trimingham Railway Station. The Station Master's house can be seen on the right and the signal box is visible at extreme left.

as it crossed bridge No. 337. The station itself was a sizeable and attractive building with a platform long enough to accommodate an express. The facilities were housed in two separate blocks under a single roof. The block nearest the steps housed the Booking Office, the bicycle storage, the Station Master's Office and a large General Waiting Room. The block to the west held the Ladies Waiting Room and Lavatory, the Porter's Room, a room each for lamps and coal, and the Gentlemen's Lavatory. A signal box stood further down the platform and a small plantation and garden were planted directly in front of the station. The sizeable yard and two sidings lay beyond. Leading Porter Billy Secker won a number of awards for Best Kept Station.

Trimingham Railway Station about 1910

Following a meeting at Liverpool Street station it was in November 1952 that the Parish Council first received news of the forthcoming closure of the railway. Initially it was to close on March 5th 1953 but the date slipped to April 6th 1953. The *Eastern Daily Press* reported rather whimsically the following day that 'the Mundesley-Cromer coast railway line, the "Garden of Sleep Railway," went into its final slumber last night.' I remember the final train to run through Trimingham. A 55-year-old tank engine pulled four coaches, carrying approximately 100 passengers. Billy Secker, the sole remaining member of staff at the station placed detonators on the line through the station yard to give the train a suitable send-off.

With many people reliant on the railway for work, shopping and for visits to the doctor in Mundesley, closure of the railway was a real blow. At the annual parish meeting when details were given of the bus service that would take the place of the rail service Rev. Arthur Buxton was moved to describe the alternative as 'shabby.' He had a point.

People accustomed to travelling on an early train to Norwich would not in future arrive in the city until 9.35 a.m. There was no daily service for people wishing to shop in Cromer. Anyone in need of the doctor in Mundesley would have to leave Trimingham at about 8 o'clock in the morning. They would arrive almost an hour before the surgery opened. On Wednesdays they could return at 11.42 a.m. On Tuesdays and Fridays they would need to remain patient until they could return at 2.00 p.m. On Mondays and Thursdays canteens and iron rations would be essential since they would be stuck until 4.55 p.m. The shortest straw however was reserved for the unfortunates that needed to see the doctor on a Saturday. They would be marooned in Mundesley from shortly after 8 o'clock in the morning until 6.50 in the evening.

Plainly, Rev. Buxton was right. The council sent a letter to the Eastern Counties Omnibus Company outlining the inadequacy of the bus service. The Company replied that it was prepared to augment the service as necessary, if there was a demand. The traffic manager added that the service between Cromer and Mundesley operated at a loss. He felt sure that the people of Trimingham would appreciate his desire not to run further uneconomic mileage.

The difficulties with the buses were not new. In April 1948 the Parish Council was asked to see whether a late bus from Cromer could be arranged on a Saturday evening. Such a service was arranged but for some time it left Cromer before most entertainments concluded.

In 1954 the council looked into the possibility of erecting a modest bus shelter at the Crown and Anchor. One could be built for £60; however the plan was shelved in March 1956.

In May 1956 the Parish Council was asked whether there was a possibility of the old railway station being purchased for use as a youth club. Many difficulties existed apparently, not the least of which turned out to be that the building had already been disposed of to someone else.

The railway station and its environs played an important part in my life during the 1950s and early 60s. It was from the station in the early 50s that we set out by steam train to visit relatives in Leamington Spa and Gloucester. The latter trip was memorable on two counts. As soon as we boarded the train I leaned out of the window and wiped both hands in an extravagant arc across the outside of the compartment door. Mother spent the next half-hour trying to remove greasy soot from my hands and coat sleeves by the old stratagem so beloved of mothers, licking and dabbing with a tiny handkerchief that was far from up to the job. Worse though was father's aberration in taking us all on the Underground to Waterloo for our connecting train instead of going to Paddington. We were almost at Gloucester on a much later train than had been intended before mother could bring herself to speak to him again.

In the early 1950s there were several notable landmarks in the station yard. Mr Skerret-Rogers' hen run was on the left just inside the gate. We talked occasionally of raiding the hen house for eggs but we never actually put a plan into operation.

The vegetable garden for Station House was on the right of the gate, conveniently out of sight of the house. To our considerable joy Mr Juby grew splendid fruit and vegetables. A few gooseberry and currant bushes grew opposite, beside what I thought for years were called the 'kettle-pins.' Billy Secker, the leading porter, was forever telling us to 'stay off them kettle-pins, together.' It was the defunct cattle pens to which he referred. In the past cattle had been herded into pens on a platform by a siding for ease of loading into cattle trucks.

Just before the railway closed a troop train of about six carriages was shunted into a siding in the station yard. We opened one of the doors without too much difficulty and made several covert but interesting visits to the train. The compartments were ankle deep and the tables overflowing with evidence of Bacchanalian excess on a grand scale. The train was a sea of beer bottles, and here and there was the odd miniature bottle of spirits. There were discarded cigarette packets, racy magazines and newspapers. Evidence of such rabid intemperance impressed us no end. Once we grew accustomed to the taste of stale light ale, Forest

Brown, whisky, rum, crisps and biscuits we had a couple of days in which to indulge ourselves before a team of cleaners moved in.

Beyond the cattle pens was the main body of the station yard with a cart road, a couple of sidings and a broad area of grass and gravel that at times hosted mountains of sugar beet, coke and coal. Once the railway closed, the yard became a playground that saw much football and cricket, the annual November 5th bonfire and ultimately, and to the eventual regret of each one of us a cycle speedway track. Our track was much longer than the norm. One could really get up a good speed on the straights... before crashing and tumbling off on one of the bends. Striving for authenticity we deliberately dressed the bends with loose sand and gravel.

I suspect that we erstwhile gladiators all carry the scars even today. I got off pretty lightly with not much more than a broken nose. For quite some time fractures, gashes, bruises and gravel rash became the norm.

On Cromer Road (still the B1159) the old Station Master's House and two Railway Cottages that once backed onto the railway station yard stand opposite the comparatively newly named St John's Meadow. All three railway properties were built originally for what now seems a very reasonable £380. While the railway was still functioning an engine driver by the name of Mr Juby lived at Station House. I well remember him at an upstairs window, his face contorted with rage on the sole occasion that we scrumped apples from the trees in his back garden. The apples were misshapen, full of grubs and unbelievably sour.

Billy Secker, who in the latter days of the railway was the sole custodian of the station and its environs, lived in the first of the Railway Cottages with his wife Blanche. As we grew into our teens we spent a good deal of time in a small hut fashioned from railway sleepers in his back yard. His grandson, Derek, was part of our merry band so we enjoyed largely unlimited access to Mr Secker's garden and beyond it the station yard. Billy Secker eventually retired aged 65 after 48 years of service with the railway. It seems a strange thing to remember but he was the only person that I ever saw who smoked Robin cigarettes.

After the Graver family moved out, a railway guard by the name of Harry Bramley moved into the other Railway Cottage. His son John was another member of our group. The family arrived in the village from Lincolnshire in the early 1950s. Beside the Bramleys' garden was Pearson's orchard. In season it provided us with a variety of apples. There were blackcurrants too but they held little appeal. Most of the apples were unremarkable but there was one tree that I remember with particular fondness. Occasionally the sheer volume of fruit on the trees ensured that at least some of it was fit to eat when we got our grubby hands on it. We discovered that when ripe, the apples on this particular tree were delicious. Purple in colour, they were hard, crunchy, juicy and sweet. They were without comparison. In appearance they were quite unlike any other apple that we had ever seen. In our ignorance we called them New Zealand apples. Sadly that apple tree was rooted up along with everything else in the orchard to make way for the Staden Park development. I've never seen apples like those 'New Zealand apples' since.

British Rail sold the land upon which the station yard stood in 1965. In addition to the station yard and Pearson's orchard, Page's pit and the field in which Norman Page kept chickens were also taken. C. S. Gray (Builders) Ltd from Mundesley commenced work on the site that would become Staden Park in 1967/68.

Beyond the railway bridge that stood above the station the road heads towards Southrepps, passing Green Lane on the left and the entrance to Buck's Heath or Keeper's Lane on the right. I was a fairly frequent visitor to Keeper's Cottage at the far end of the lane in the late 1950s. The Reynolds family moved there when Percy Reynolds became gamekeeper for the Buxton estate. The previous incumbent was Billy Marling. He had been a familiar sight around the woods and lanes in his cap, cords and leather gaiters. During 1959 Gabriel, Wade and English built a deep litter house close to the Keeper's Cottage. My father helped erect that house and when it was completed he joined the company and went off round the country building barns.

As children we used to do a circuit about once a year, walking from Middle Street along Green Lane, down Keeper's Lane and on by way of Clapham Dams Farm. We returned past the beck and up the Southrepps road or by way of the Sidestrand S-bends and the coast road. Whichever way we chose, it was a tidy step and we invariably stopped at Clapham Dams for a drink of water from the pump, which is still there. The house at Clapham Dams has a couple of stones high on the wall. The first is inscribed RW 1801, probably after R. Wortley who presumably built the house in 1801. The second stone carries the initials EGH for Edward Harrison who renovated the property in 1996.

15. The Vexed Question of a Playing Field.

Following a Parish Meeting on December 4th 1894 the village elders applied to the County Council for the appointment of a Parish Council for Trimingham. The first meeting of that august body took place on January 18th 1895. The most pressing matter on the agenda was gaining permission from the Buxtons to use the school classroom as a public library. The council established a parish charity that same year, intending to raise funds for agricultural labourers belonging to, or born in the parish.

Emboldened by obtaining permission to use the school for an annual meeting and for Parish Council meetings, the new council then addressed a thorny problem that exercised elements of the village for well over a century. They applied to Mr T. F. Buxton to use the White Cross Pightle to the west of White Gate Lane, rent free, as a recreation ground. Regretfully Mr Buxton felt unable to grant use of the land for that purpose. Nor was he inclined, in subsequent approaches, to rent it.

The question of a playing field arose again and again. It was back on the agenda in 1946 when the council instructed the clerk to approach Rev. Buxton to see whether he could help obtain a field from Mr Harrison. In the meantime thanks were due to Robert Page for allowing the Football Club to use his field for the forthcoming season.

Three years later the problem hadn't been resolved. The Council considered approaching the National Playing Fields Association. They identified Mr Page's field behind the church as a suitable patch of ground for a football pitch. The football club was prepared to pay rent and remove the goalposts after each game. However in 1950 Mr Page refused the use of his field for football or any other recreation. He said that it was the only field that he had available for grazing.

The same year the council received the offer of a piece of land opposite the Crown and Anchor Hotel between Gavelkind and Middle Street, for use as a recreation ground. Mr H. Royce offered it to the parish for about £250, the same price that he had paid to purchase it. He wished to retain the road frontage but otherwise had roughly 5 acres available. The Ministry of Education would grant roughly 50% of the purchase price. The balance could be raised in the form of a long-term loan, repayable by a small sum annually over 30 or 40 years. The council intended soliciting ideas for fund-raising, although if necessary the repayment could be recovered in the parish rates. They called a Parish Meeting to discuss the matter. Representatives from the Women's Institute, the Bowls Club, the Football Club and the Men's Club attended the meeting. It was felt that even if the Agricultural Executive Committee would not agree to the ground being used for the purposes of recreation for some time the purchase should proceed anyway.

Somehow much of this enthusiasm evaporated. Less than six months later the lack of response to a request for assistance in raising funds led to Mr Skerret-Rogers, then chairman of the council, declaring his unhappiness about proceeding. He needed more assurance that a playing field was really wanted. He should have sought input from the youth of the village. I was only six or so at the time but along with a number of other youngsters had already been picked to make up the number in teams to play both cricket and football against Gimingham and Southrepps. Both villages had their own playing field. We had to play our home games in a field of stubble. The youth and children of the village were desperate for a playing field.

The sorry saga continued. In March 1951 the proposed site was still available but the council chairman remained unconvinced. He wanted more interest from the parishioners and the appointment of a committee. However, neither the Men's Club nor the village as a whole would support the Social Club's activities. Stating that he spoke from experience, the ever-helpful Rev. Abigail added that in his opinion the scheme was altogether too ambitious.

Entirely predictably, a year later the owner of the field withdrew his offer. The council minutes recorded lack of local support. The matter was considered closed. Fat chance!

In 1959 the Parish Council approached Norwich Education Committee for permission for the local children to use the playing field on Gimingham Hill when it was not in use by Norwich children. A full year later, permission was refused. When I lived in Middle Street one of the highlights of the summer was the visit of the Boys' Brigade from Norwich to the Education Committee field on Gimingham Hill for their annual camp. Anticipation began to build from the moment we heard the first bugle over the hill. On the Sunday morning of their visit we were all agog waiting for the first crash of drums as they set out from camp to march through the village to church parade. By the time they were swinging past the Crown and Anchor we were at the bottom of Middle Street craning

Norwich Education Community Hut on Gimingham Hill, exterior, in the 1950s

The interior of the hut. The Boys Brigade from Norwich camped here each summer

Photos courtesy of Norfolk County Council Library & Information Service

our necks to watch them pass. Sometimes we followed them all the way to the church.

In December 1971 the vexed question of a playing field was again raised, only to be left once more. The subject returned to the front burner in 1975. Again it was left in abeyance due to lack of interest, cost, the original site being on the route of a proposed bypass, and the alternative site being too close to the road.

Today there is a playing field and children's play area, but in numerous visits I have never seen a soul making use of it. Located on the seaward side of the Cromer Road behind a number of new houses in the comparatively recently named St John's Meadow, it is apparently used from time to time, but not for any organised sporting activities.

Between the playing field and the cliff stands a rectangle of woodland that we referred to as the Fir Wood. When I was a child an avenue of conifers ran the entire length of the woods. I believe that they were felled en masse during the storms of the late 1980s. In early 2007 plenty of trees remain but conifers are represented by only two misshapen pines on the southern edge of the wood.

Certainly in the early and mid 1900s there was an obvious and identifiable need for a playing field. Goodness knows why the landowners and the council of the time were unable to acknowledge it and work together to meet the requirement. A playing field would have been much used. One has to conclude that for much of the last hundred years or so there was on the part of some of the people that had the wherewithal to make a real difference, a distinct lack of will.

In many respects the time for a playing field has probably passed. Today, parental anxiety about letting young children play outside unsupervised is not difficult to understand and there is no shortage of activities for children either at home or within an easy car ride. A bare and windswept patch of grass on the cliff tops probably appears one of the less inviting options available to both parents and children today.

16. Cromer Road, the Watch House and the Slussman's Lane Battle Area

On April 1st 1925, G. Deary and W. Pardon attended the Parish Council meeting as applicants for the first two council houses to be built beside the Cromer Road at the west end of the village. A year later the council applied for two further council houses. They recommended H. Payne and B. Fuller to the Rural District Council as suitable tenants. Harry Payne was still in residence when we moved into one of four more council houses in 1952.

During the early 1930s the small field upon which the council houses now stand was the site of an unusual occurrence. Periodically a small red and white aeroplane landed there. A woman, thought to have some connection with Wills, the tobacco people, piloted the plane. Whatever else the purpose of her visit she brought with her tobacco for Frank Allard, who at the time lived at Lilac Cottage in Church Street. After a brief visit the plane took to the air again, heading across the fields towards the sea.

Beside the council houses White Gate Lane runs from the Cromer Road towards the sea. The original lane is somewhat truncated these days, having been rerouted diagonally across the field behind the houses and through the Fir Woods to the cliffs. When I was a child the lane turned to the west after a hundred yards or so. It continued to the Pond Plantation and then veered off towards the sea. During the mid 19th century the lane forked near the Duck Decoy Pond. The seaward leg was known as the Driftway and ran to the west of the Watch House and the Watch House Plantation. The other leg continued in a westerly direction through Pond Plantation and Nut Copse until it rejoined the Cromer Road beside Osier Carr.

The Laborious Plantation and chalk pit that were on the cliff top just to the west of White Gate Lane at the end of the 19th century are no more. They and the Sea Plantation and Nursery to the east of the lane were lost to erosion long ago. One wonders why the Laborious Plantation was so named. Did the planting involve great exertion or take a long time? The cliffs below and into Sidestrand were known as the Low Grounds.

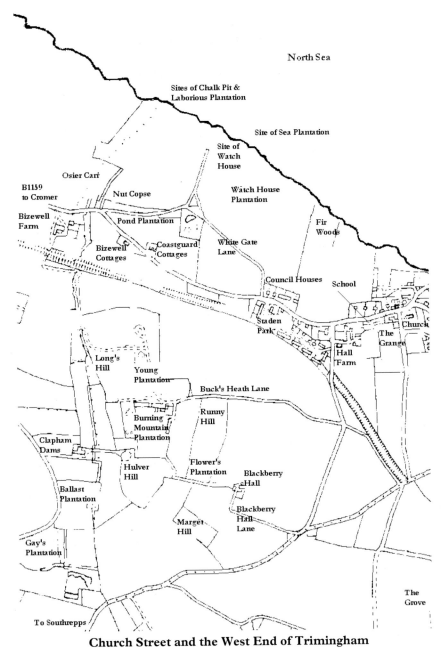

Church Street and the West End of Trimingham

Reproduced by permission of the Ordnance Survey on behalf of HMSO © Crown Copyright 2007. All rights reserved. Ordnance Survey Licence number 46946

100

During the 19th century a Watch House was erected on the cliff tops just to the east of White Gate Lane. It probably came into operation in 1841 since a stone marker bearing the legend 'Watch House 1841,' was recovered comparatively recently from a local garden.

It is likely that some provision for assistance to mariners existed much earlier. In 1807 George W. Manby, barrack-master at Great Yarmouth, first succeeded in projecting a line over a stranded vessel. The following year he saved a crew of seven from a vessel foundering 150 yards from the beach. He was instrumental in saving many lives with his invention.

In 1813 Manby issued a 'General Report on the Survey of the Eastern Coast of England – for establishing the system for saving shipwrecked persons.' At Trimingham Manby found that 'the shooting down of immense masses of cliff has greatly assisted in creating outer sands, an evil which I find increasing, and which renders it necessary to have a 5½ inch brass mortar, with a 6 pound mortar to be promptly forwarded to Mundsley to prevent reoccurrences of the fatal accidents that have occurred from the mortar of Hasborough not arriving in time.'

The level of fishing and other maritime activity in the area led to the full-time presence of H. M. Preventive Service in Trimingham. Up to five boatmen or coastguards lived in the village in the mid 1800s. The Watch House was said to be a large barn-like building with double doors at one end. It contained apparatus for launching rockets to anyone in distress in the sea, with a lifebelt and line attached. A signal staff stood nearby. The rocket apparatus remained on the cliff top for communicating with distressed vessels after the Preventive Service was withdrawn in 1883. The concrete base could still be seen when I was a child.

★

The military used the seaward end of White Gate Lane and the surrounding cliff tops for battle training during both wars. A decade after the end of the 2nd World War the area became the scene of much feverish activity on the part of the youth of the village. By the late 1950s there was scarcely a boy that didn't have, secreted about his parents' property, a cache of live ammunition.

Searching the banks and ditches we unearthed live .303 ammunition, smoke and mortar bombs. Most of these items accompanied us home, clanking and jingling in sacks and jacket pockets. Heart failure would have been rife if our parents had known the full extent of the explosives hidden about their properties.

The .303 ammunition was easily dismantled. However the powder or cordite from within invariably flared in a disappointing fashion when lit. It wasn't nearly as good as a penny banger from Alice's shop. But we lacked

**A member of the Bomb Disposal Unit displays
a selection of ordnance, 1950s**
Photo: Courtesy of Archant Norfolk Photographic

the application and imagination of the following generation. Or perhaps it was simply that we were less foolhardy. Boys younger than us built a bonfire beneath a mound of mortar bombs. They dropped them from the top of stepladders onto concrete paths and threw them about with abandon. Fortunately none exploded. One child was discovered setting about a live bomb with a hammer and chisel in his father's bench vice. I forget how it all ended. So far as I am aware everyone survived this foolishness.

White Gate Lane was known to many of the locals as Slussman's Lane, apparently because it was rarely free of 'sluss' or mud. It was certainly the case in the 1950s and 60s. In 1957 the Parish Council received complaints about silage dumps. One such dump fouled the air midway down White Gate Lane. Liquid from the silage formed malodorous brown pools in the rutted lane. The silage dumps were considered by some to be a nuisance but little could be done since the smell was not actually prejudicial to public health. It was all part of living in the countryside.

The same had been true of living with bird scarers. Operating these devices throughout the night in the summer of 1958 brought complaints and a letter to ERDC. By the end of the year Norfolk County Council had adopted a by-law prohibiting the use of bird scarers during the hours of darkness.

There seems to be some possibility that White Gate Lane may be reinstated in the future.

★

In the mid 1960s there was a proposal for a new road to bypass Trimingham. I had left the village by this time but I remember there being a certain amount of interest, surprise and even joy. As late as 1968 there was still some faith in the project. Gradually the initial reaction was replaced by pessimism and ultimately a firm belief on the part of most folk that it would never come to pass within their lifetime. Heavy traffic through the village prompted the Parish Council to ask ERDC when a start on the bypass was envisaged since it was much needed. By November 1974 there remained no movement on the project. The same appears to be the case today.

Beyond the council houses the Cromer Road rises in a westerly direction to the top of Buildings Hill. The hill was so named after The Buildings, situated half way down the far side of the hill on the right and later known as Coastguard Cottages.

During the mid 1920s and 1930s the Parish Council spent a good deal of time debating the roads. They approached the AA for signs and in 1927 requested that the road from the council houses towards Sidestrand be widened since it contained a dangerous 'S' bend. They reported that the problem still hadn't been resolved a full ten years later. Nearly eighty years on the 'S' bend remains, still not appreciably wider than it ever was, but most people manage to negotiate it without too much difficulty.

At the top of Buildings Hill is the entrance to Woodland Leisure Park. It occupies almost 50 acres of woodland, once part of the Buxton estate. The park offers services and accommodation for touring caravans and caravan holiday homes. The Clubhouse is built on the site of the old Keeper's Cottage and is named after Billy Marling, the gamekeeper. The approach to the park is by means of a private drive through woods and farmland, crossing the site of the now levelled railway cutting through which once ran the line between Trimingham and Overstrand. In the 1950s the railway embankments there were smothered in gorse and brambles. It was a good place to pick blackberries and wild strawberries.

Beyond the entrance to Woodland Leisure Park the B1159 descends to the parish boundary. It is no wider than it was over fifty years ago and with the same steep and unforgiving banks on either side. As a child I saw a small black Austin perched at least five feet up on one of those banks.

Down the hill, Coastguard Cottages, once four dwellings, are now three. H.M. Preventive Service boatmen and coastguards lived there during the mid 1800s. J. H. Buxton built the Bizewell Cottages opposite in 1900, but it is probable that they were built on the site of earlier dwellings.

At the foot of the hill, Green's Belt lies on the left beside Bizewell Farmhouse, and Osier Carr stands on the right of the coast road as one takes leave of Trimingham. Bizewell Farmhouse itself is not within the parish boundary. It was built in 1754 of brick, flint and tile. In October 1963 it was put up for sale as a corn and stock farm of 113.868 acres. It was part of the Trimingham Residential and Sporting Estate put on the market by Michael Auriol Buxton of Field Dalling.

When we were children Green's Belt was the place to go for bamboo. We used it to make dens, spears and arrows. It was suited to none of these purposes. It was easy to work with but too flimsy for successful den-making. One could make something that resembled a spear but it would never fly straight and who really wants a spear anyway? The arrows were lethal. Any attempt to fire one from a bow invariably ripped the skin from the soft flesh between thumb and forefinger.

Osier Carr is a 0.4 acre plot of woodland opposite Bizewell Farm on the western border of the parish. It was given 'for the poor of the parish not in receipt of Poor Law relief.' Funds raised from the rent of the land were intended to provide something for the poor of the parish once every three years. In 1943 it was registered as a charity and rented out at 17s. per annum until 1987. At Christmas 1954 the charity trustees delivered 1 cwt of coal to 15 parishioners.

Beyond Osier Carr lies Sidestrand and robber barons, mean spirits and dragons.

17. 'A fine beach with good bathing and walks along the cliffs.'

The people of North Norfolk have always had a close relationship with the sea. A lengthy coastline, availability of resources and the relative flatness of the land presented considerable potential for transport, trade and recreation. The area offered opportunities to settle, work and play that proved irresistible to many folk.

In the early 16th century Cromer was a port with 30 ships, fishing and trading for the most part with Norway and Iceland. 117 householders and 48 mariners and fishermen lived in the town. It had a landing place called 'the peere', and encroachment of the sea was recognised as a problem even then. In 1551 the people of Cromer petitioned the Privy Council for help in protecting the town. Some 30 years later they were enabled by licence to collect dues on wheat, barley and malt. The money rebuilt the pier and provided sea defences. By the 19th century Cromer was importing coal, tiles, oil cake and porter in vessels of 60-100 tons burthen. There were four curing houses and many of the inhabitants were fishermen.

Sheringham had 136 householders and 69 mariners and fishermen in the 16th century. It had a landing place known as 'the hythe'. Three hundred years later Lower Sheringham was still a busy fishing station with 6 curing houses and 26 fishing boats. A visitor observed that 'a peep down the cliffs is enough to strike a stranger with horror, although the farmers often plough to the very brink.' Goodness knows what he would have made of the cliffs at Trimingham had he ventured so far.

'Mondislie' also boasted a landing place in 1565. There 16 householders and 19 fishermen dwelt in the town, making a living from herring and mackerel fishing. By the mid 19th century, in addition to becoming a bathing place, Mundesley was importing coal and timber and exporting corn. There were 4 large boats fishing for herring and 7 small boats fishing for crabs, lobsters and cod.

Singular or not, we know that a hamlet or village of some sort has existed in the vicinity of Trimingham and Beacon Hill since the 11th century. Indeed a hill of that height and its proximity to the sea would have been significant factors in the establishment of any early settlement. Given the proliferation of boats around the coast at the time it is almost certain that men worked from the beach at Trimingham during the 16th century. The families of Clipperton and Cubitt were certainly engaged in fishing during the 17th and 18th centuries and they would not have been alone. From the mid 1800s there were at least seven fishermen working from the beach. Members of the families of Olley, Allard, Bullimore and Pardon joined the Clippertons and Cubitts.

A number of local men and women made the trip to Scarborough to join the fleet of drifters that set out annually from the north of Scotland in pursuit of herring. John Bullimore made the trip in 1861 and for many more years. William and Mary Cubitt, Francis Allard, George Pardon and others joined him in 1881. These fishing folk stayed with the vessels as they worked their way south down the North Sea to Great Yarmouth.

During a herring glut tons of fish were spread on some of the fields in Trimingham as manure.

The last fishermen working from Trimingham beach just before 2nd World War were Tom Kidd and his boat *'Ethel'*, Tom and Theo Clarke with *'The Two Brothers'*, the Deary *'Marigold'*, and George Clarke and the *'Mayflower'*.

Henry Kirk, Tom and Theo Clarke launch the *'Two Brothers'* from the beach at Trimingham.

On a tour through the eastern counties in the 1720s Daniel Defoe was mightily impressed by the risks run by seamen off Norfolk. He made reference to a terrible storm in 1682 in which 200 corn ships and colliers were lost in a single night between Cromer and Great Yarmouth.

Defoe also spotted the local penchant for beach-combing. A number of the older buildings in Trimingham contain materials bearing evidence of maritime origin. Old ships' timbers are still doing service today in the form of beams, joists, posts and planking.

Of the coast off Cromer and north of Winterton, Defoe remarked that 'the farmers and country people had scarce a barn or shed, or a stable, nay, not the pales of their yards and gardens, not a hogstye, not a necessary-house, but what was built of old planks, beams, wales and timbers etc., the wrecks of ships and ruins of mariners' and merchants' fortunes, and some places were whole yards filled and piled up very high with the same stuff laid up, as I supposed, to sell for the like building purposes, as there should be occasion.'

Had he been alive in the 1950s and 60s Defoe would probably have been unsurprised to see that the practise was still pursued with much vigour. Father was only one of a number of men who built entire sheds and pieces of furniture with what they could bring home from the beach tied to the crossbars of their bicycles. On occasion these bold adventurers had to dodge the constable on the cliff top, but apparently that wasn't too challenging. Most of them had one or two favoured places where they could conceal their haul while they waited for a more opportune time to spirit it home.

On a couple of memorable occasions the beach became temporarily a beach-comber's paradise. Once in the early 1950s the shore was littered with new pit-props. There was an earlier occasion when the sands were smothered with Jaffa oranges. There were even complete boxes of fruit to be had by the early bird. Jack Olley was recalling those events only recently. His face took on a wistful look and I spotted a slight mistiness in his eye as he spoke. It was the very same look that came over father at the mention of pit-props or oranges. Two of the sheds that father built in the 1950s from driftwood remain in use today.

Father brought home many treasures from the beach. Lead weights, tangles of net and line, 'interesting' shells, stones and pieces of fossilised bone. The bones of horses, deer, elephants, mammoths, hippopotami and bison have been found on the beach. Father returned from one beach-combing expedition with an Iron Age spear that he had recovered whole from the Forest Bed. After examination at Norwich Castle Museum it was consigned to a corner in our hall for years. One night it succumbed to the inexorable advance of corrosion and the pull of gravity. The following morning we found it in pieces on the hall floor.

★

Holidaymakers once flocked to Trimingham. On holiday at Garden Cottage in 1910 Charlie and Edie sent a postcard of Marl Point to a friend in Hampstead. 'Having a nice time here, weather is rather cool and very windy, but fine and dry. It's a very pretty place. We are 300 or 400 feet above the sea. We have been blackberry picking.' A surprising number of visitors to Trimingham wrote about enjoying their holidays picking blackberries.

It is true that Trimingham is situated on the highest cliffs in North Norfolk, but Edie was mistaken; the Beacon is actually 226 feet above sea level. High as the cliffs are, the soft heterogeneous glacial deposits make them among the most unstable in the county. Their low shear strength makes them vulnerable to wave erosion and failure caused by undercutting. The cliffs are subject to frequent falls and are regarded as the finest site of slumping unconsolidated sediments in Britain. They also offer dramatic views which are unequalled anywhere else in Norfolk. Interestingly there were times when parts of the cliff remained sufficiently stable to allow farmer Chris Harrison to graze cattle on some of the less steep slopes.

Over the centuries many acres of land and entire buildings have been lost to erosion. It has always been difficult to maintain even a semi-permanent way down the cliffs to the beach. Two farmhouses and several acres of land were washed away in 1822. In *'A General History of the County of Norfolk'* in 1829, John Stacy recorded the incident.

'The overflowing of the sea makes every year a powerful impression upon the scene; for what in one year stands as a bold point, projecting into the sea, in the next gives place, and is, perhaps, hollowed into a spacious bay. At Trimmingham, where one of these bays was formed to a considerable extent, not indeed by the action of the sea, but by a subterranean body of water, supposed to be collected by the choking up of a spring, two farm-houses, with their yards and outbuildings, besides several acres of land, fell a prey to the unsuspected enemy. One of these houses stood several weeks after the first had fallen, and was considered in a state of safety, till a crack in the land beyond it was discovered. Upon this separated part was a stack of hay, the removal of which was attended with singular good fortune, for the wheels of the wagon containing the last load had scarcely cleared the separated part, when the whole of it gave way.'

Mudflows and the effects of slumping are clearly visible

T. F. Buxton erected a breakwater in 1842 in an effort to stem erosion of the cliffs and the loss of glebe land into the sea. In 1883 a further six breakwaters were constructed.

From 1966 to 1985 the mean rate of erosion at Trimingham was far greater than elsewhere on the coast between Weybourne and Happisburgh. It measured over two metres per year in places, up to three or four times the rate of erosion at other locations close by.

The principal causes of erosion on the North Norfolk coast are wave action and the presence of groundwater. From Overstrand to Trimingham there are numerous examples of rotational failures and mudslides that have been influenced by groundwater. The cliffs become better drained and more stable towards Mundesley.

The sand and gravel components in the cliffs are permeable. However, impermeable clays can intercept water percolating through the cliffs causing it to pond and discharge at the cliff face. This can take the form of small mudflows or slumps or large mudslides and deep-seated rotational failures. The latter are capable of removing up to ¼ million cubic meters of material at a time. Large failures induced by groundwater have occurred comparatively often at Trimingham.

Cliff failures purely from wave erosion tend to be small but frequent. Wave action rapidly removes fallen material from the base of the cliffs, so that the cliff face is maintained at a steep, unstable angle and prone to further failures.

In addition to mass movement three other aspects of the geology of the area are of particular interest: the Pleistocene sediments, the chalk, and fossil invertebrates. The cliffs at both Trimingham and Sidestrand exhibit a fine series of geological exposures in unconsolidated Pleistocene sediments and underlying chalk. Dr Jane Hart (University of Southampton) is of the view that the entirety of the Sidestrand-Trimingham section is involved in a deformation event which she has named the 'Trimingham disturbance.' It is characterised by large-scale open folding resulting from horizontal forces or pro-glacial thrusting.

The chalk that has been exposed on the foreshore and in the cliffs has been thrust upwards as a series of blocks by glacial action. These chalk exposures are of Lower Maastrichtian age and are the only significant example of chalk of this age in Britain. They are also the youngest Mesozoic rocks in the British Isles. Analysis of the cliffs has led to a detailed picture of early Pleistocene environments and it has yielded some interesting mammalian fauna. The cliffs form probably the best site for fossil invertebrates in East Anglia.

★

In 1909 a visitor sent a postcard from Trimingham showing tents and bathers on the beach at the foot of a steep and winding pathway down the cliff. 'This is our best way down to the sea,' wrote E. W. 'The sands are lovely...when you get there.' In the 1930s Don wrote to Mr Morris at Radlett saying that 'we have to walk ¼ mile to the beach, but the bathing is good.'

The Beach at Trimingham in 1909

In 1932 the Parish Council erected a notice board on the cliff top in response to the large amount of refuse being dumped over the cliff edge. The problem still hadn't gone away in 1937 when they came to the conclusion that the parish was in dire need of a rubbish tip.

Before the 2nd World War the wide, flat sandy beach was very popular with holidaymakers. Bathing machines had been introduced in Cromer and Mundesley as early as the end of the 1700s. Tents and eventually huts were in use at Sheringham. The cliffs were too steep for bathing machines at Trimingham so bathers used tents instead. For some time a pleasure steamer put in at the beach en route between Cromer and Gt Yarmouth.

In March 1945 the Parish Council was in receipt of information concerning government loans for holiday resorts. They were unable to come up with any projects for which a loan was required.

A member of the Parish Council wondered in 1958 whether it was necessary for farmers to plough so near the cliff edge. Since the farmers must be aware of the grave risk that they ran in so doing, it was concluded that there was no satisfactory answer to this question.

In 1965, St J. D. Buxton recalled holidays that the family took in Trimingham at the end of the 19th century. The three boys, Mademoiselle and his mother took the train from London to North Walsham. From there their journey continued by horse and wagonette to a primitive cottage in a seaside village where his mother found the lack of sanitation something of a trial. She became exasperated at the need to boil a large black kettle in order to clean the boys. His mother was a keen bather so his father set up a bell tent on the shore. The boys bought ginger nuts and enormous bulls-eyes at the village shop.

The level of the beach is very variable. 'Strangers should note that a shallow depression lies between the beach and the sands and that on an incoming tide non-swimmers are liable to find themselves out of their depth.' In their *Illustrated Guide Book for North Norfolk*, Ward Lock & Co. felt it necessary to sound a cautionary note. It was probably true, at least until the next tide when the beach profile could change beyond recognition.

The North Sea Action Group (NSAG) was formed by Broadland (later Norfolk) Friends of the Earth in conjunction with Great Yarmouth Trades Council. Since the 1980s NSAG has been successful in raising public awareness of the impact of offshore dredging on erosion and the consequent decay of the coastline and marine environment. It is felt that dredging operations have led to changes in sea-flow patterns, deepening the offshore seabed and permitting greater waves which have led to an increase in the slope of beaches by the drawdown of sand and shingle.

Working on sea defences at Trimingham

Today a wooden revetment and groynes provide a degree of protection to the parish. The revetment was constructed on a concrete apron to provide a firm foundation. As early as 1980 there was extensive damage to the structure, brought about by cliff falls. By July 1982 it was reported that roughly 30% of the revetment had gone, broken by cliff falls and washed away. Certainly some of the revetment has been destroyed and beach levels have dropped, exposing the concrete apron. This has created a scouring effect leading to further beach erosion. The concrete apron is acting as a sea wall, a purpose for which it was not designed. It has suffered severe damage as a consequence but the parish has insufficient assets at risk for any realistic chance of repair or replacement of the sea defences.

Expert opinion now prefers abandonment of the traditional methods of sea defence on the North Norfolk coast in favour of a 'managed retreat.' In a coastal defence blueprint by North Norfolk and other interested district councils experts propound the view that the sole affordable and sustainable way to manage the coast is to let nature take its course. Professor T. O'Riordan, an environmental scientist at the University of East Anglia, is reported as saying, 'Building more concrete walls will just end in tears. They are a waste of time and money. Defences save only cliff top properties; they actually destroy coastlines. We must make a mobile and unstable coast.'

Building new sea defences at Trimingham was not always straightforward

Understandably this notion is not popular with the cliff top dwellers. They tend to view the lack of concrete walls as a more likely cause of misery. Many see the probability of a drop in the value of their properties. Others however, face the likelihood of losing their homes, their businesses, their land, their very community, and all within the foreseeable future.

A cliff fall causes another setback in building sea defences

18. Tales of the Sea

A number of seamen, vessels and bathers have come to an untimely end on the shore at Trimingham. In the 19th century it was a common enough occurrence. On at least five occasions in the 1830s the body of a drowned sailor was found on the beach. Four more unfortunates were washed ashore in the 1850s.

On November 5th 1881 the following report appeared in the *Norfolk Chronicle and Norwich Gazette*.

TRIMINGHAM - SAD TALE OF THE SEA

On Sunday last a Dutch fishing boat was discovered ashore by Mr. Robert Dye, a fisherman, residing here, and after the church service was over in the afternoon a number of fishermen and others went on the beach, and a hole was made in the bottom, when the bodies of five men and two boys were found in the cabin. They were drawn out with ropes and laid on the beach, where they remained until the morning (it being impossible to carry them off, on account of there being no gangway for carts, and the cliffs being too steep to permit of their being carried), when two carts were sent round by Mundesley and the bodies were laid thereon, and brought here and put into a building belonging to Mr. Samuel Cubitt. The coroner was communicated with, and it was expected an inquest would be held, but the decomposed state of the bodies did not permit of their being kept longer than Tuesday afternoon, when they were put in coffins made for them by Mr. George Cubitt, and buried in the churchyard in two graves. The Rev. H. Matchett read the service in a most impressive manner, a number of persons being present. Men are now being employed in getting the cargo out of the boat, which consists of a great quantity of herring in barrels, fishing nets &c. All the rigging &c. of the boat appears to have been blown away, and the boat lies flat upon the beach, nearly opposite the beacon. It is presumed that the boat capsized during the recent gale whilst riding at anchor.

The vessel that foundered was a large flat-bottomed Dutch fishing smack named *De Vrouw Arendje* from Katwijk aan Zee. It was thought likely that the vessel perished during a gale on October 14th. Robert Olley and William Deary were the men who broke through the hull and recovered the fully clothed bodies of the crew. Mr Deary was unwell for some time after the discovery.

The people of Trimingham buried the bodies in the churchyard on November 1st 1881 and erected a stone to mark the grave. Mrs S. E. Matchett, wife of the Rector, Rev. Abraham Matchett, wrote the following tribute to the crew of *De Vrouw Arendje*. The poem was lent to the Rector, Rev. D. G. Townsend by Mrs W. Olley of Rotunda Cottage in 1943.

A Tale of the Sea

Afloat on the sea, the Smiling Sea
The little bark rides merrily,
And mother and wife by the Cottage door
Wave a fond adieu as she leaves the shore.

Over the sea, the Sparkling Sea
The little bark speeds merrily.
The skipper and crew lose sight of the shore
Of the friends and home they're to see no more.

Over the sea, the dancing sea
The little bark skims merrily.
The Silvery herrings come dancing by
And soon they will haul a good supply
That will comforts bring to the cottage door
To the wives and mothers that wait on shore.

Over the sea, the tossing sea
The little bark sails merrily
But the threatening clouds and the dancing swell
The gathering tempest now foretell,
And the skipper scans with anxious eye
And snow-tipped billows and rise and die.

Over the sea, the angry sea
The little bark rides heavily
The sails are furled, for the wind is high
And danger and death are drawing nigh

Over the sea, the raging sea
The little bark drives helplessly
It comes, that fatal, cruel wave,
No hand is near to help and save
That skipper bold, and his hardy hand
Will never alive, regain the land
Over the sea, the calm blue sea
There came, upturned and silently
Beneath our cliffs on our lonely shore
The little bark that shall sail no more,
And coffined in cabin, still and dark
Lay seven forms all cold and dark

Born hither by waves from a foreign land
To be laid in the earth by a stranger's hand
But watching and waiting in homes far away
Be many a wife and mother today
Or straining sad eyes as they stand on shore
Longing for those whom they'll see no more.

It is thought that the people of Katwijk remained ignorant of the whereabouts of their relatives for many years. Some descendants of the crew eventually visited Trimingham for a service held on November 1st 1981, one hundred years after the burial. It was an impressive service at which the PCC laid a wreath.

Some 119 years after the tragedy whilst on honeymoon the great grandson of the captain of *De Vrouw Arendje* visited Trimingham. He asked whether the original gravestone could be replaced with a new one. On Sunday June 30th 2002 a service was held in the church to mark both the Golden Jubilee of Queen Elizabeth II and to dedicate a new gravestone to mark the burial place of the crew of *De Vrouw Arendje*. The service was attended by some 239 people, including relatives of the crew and Dutch and English dignitaries. On a very moving occasion the people of Katwijk thanked the people of Trimingham for all that they had done for the crew of *De Vrouw Arendje*. They presented the church with a replica boat, an 1894 Dutch Bible and a History of Katwijk.

*

In August 1930 a youth, one of a Bible Class party from St Luke's Church, Norwich, was drowned in the sea at the rear of the Crown and Anchor. The party was staying at the Education Hut on Gimingham Hill. It was the third tragedy in which a Norwich man had been involved at Trimingham that year.

Photo: Courtesy of Simon Knott

On December 16th 1931 the body of Mrs Alice Ellen Wood, aged 61, from the White House, Trimingham, was found on the beach. It was concluded that she had 'drowned herself whilst in a state of unsound mind.'

On November 27th 1980, the front page of the *Eastern Daily Press* carried the story of the *Raven*, a 40 foot single-masted yacht travelling from Rochester in Kent to Goole in Yorkshire that got into difficulties off Trimingham. The headlines read 'Man missing as yacht is wrecked. One swims ashore at Trimingham.' The *Raven* ran into trouble in force 5 winds and began to sink in the early hours of November 26th. Mr M. Babbage of Hoo in Kent swam ashore and spent five hours on the beach before he was found by Mr Harold Ward of Beacon Road, Trimingham out walking his dog. Mr Babbage was taken to Cromer Hospital suffering from exposure. Despite a search by police, coastguards and a Sea King helicopter a second man, Mr M. J. Connor of Knaresborough, Yorks was never found. The remains of the *Raven* remain embedded in the sand to this day.

19. A Singular Village?

Anyone negotiating the coast road today through the narrow streets of Trimingham might be forgiven for concluding that there is little to see that is remarkable. At the eastern end of the village the Kevlon dome at the radar station on Beacon Hill might appear quite striking, especially on a bright sunny day. Conversely, on a dull day the perimeter fencing and the Arnold Shelters can seem grim and even a little menacing.

The weeds and puddles that presently furnish the otherwise bare gap between the road and the cliff tops where once stood the Crown and Anchor are hardly likely to cause comment unless one knew of the earlier existence of the once handsome hotel.

In the heart of the village the church of St John the Baptist might arouse interest since it is clearly ancient. It is also quite picturesque, set among the attractive brick and flint cottages and barn conversions in and around Church Street with the old red telephone kiosk standing sentinel beside the thatched lych gate. Both the radar station and the church are still in use, but to the passer-by there is little to hint at the richness of the roles that they once played in the community.

The village stands on the highest cliffs in Norfolk but from most vehicles little of the sea is visible other than in the vicinity of Beacon Hill. From the road it is difficult to get a true impression of the height of the cliff tops above sea level and it is impossible to appreciate the spectacular views along the coast. The cliffs and beach hold no small significance for the geologist and historian and together they are designated a site of special scientific interest.

Where once there were several paths down to the shore, today there is no easy access from within the main body of the village. The beach, for centuries the site of a small fishing industry and once so popular with holidaymakers, is seldom used today.

The entire parish stands within an area of outstanding natural beauty and the village and the surrounding countryside are certainly pleasing to the eye. One can enjoy exceptional views offshore and inland from various high points in the parish. In addition to the buildings around the church and on Church Street there are a number of other attractive properties. However the village is arguably no more picturesque than many other settlements on the North Norfolk coast. The observant might notice too that there is currently no shop, Post Office, pub or school, but this is not so unusual today.

Much ancient and a fair amount of the comparatively recent fabric and its associated history has quite literally disappeared off the face of the earth in Trimingham, removed by the frequent and often sizeable cliff falls that have plagued this part of the coast for centuries.

*

Until recent times the inhabitants of Trimingham worked both the land and the sea. Farming remains a major activity today but a change of emphasis and heavy reliance on machinery ensure that it employs few people locally. Fishing was a vital activity in the village but it was wholly dependent upon unfettered access to the beach and the sea. In the early 20th century the holiday trade was developing and becoming a valuable component of the economy of the village but it too was reliant upon the same beach access. Neither activity remained viable after the planting of land mines on the cliffs and the closing of the beach in 1940.

It was this, an unwanted claim to singularity thrust upon Trimingham, that proved so influential in shaping the village for the remainder of the century. The planting of mines in the unstable cliffs was a disaster for the village. The ramifications of that act and the subsequent delay in clearing the minefield are still felt today. The interval of 26 years before the beach re-opened proved a setback from which the village has struggled to recover.

There is now nothing to see of the years of painstaking effort and risks once taken, and the price paid in human life in order to restore the beach to public use. Also little evidence exists locally of the dramas played out during two World Wars in the waters off the village, on the cliff tops and in the air above.

While Trimingham was cursed with the distinction of possessing the last wartime minefield in the country British society was undergoing rapid change. Other seaside settlements were able to take advantage of the rebuilding, the new optimism and wealth. Far from even marking time Trimingham slid backwards. Potential holidaymakers learned that the beach was closed and that there was nowhere to stay. Without the beach the village had nothing to offer visitors. There was little enough for the natives.

The railway, another component vital to the holiday trade, closed and the village became dependent for public transport on a bus service that was often inadequate and inconvenient. So people went elsewhere and for many years Trimingham looked no more than an unremarkable place that one had to pass through on the way to somewhere else.

When the beach reopened, the cliffs remained closed to the public so there was no practical means of access. Given these circumstances, together with the legendary instability of the cliffs and the existing availability of facilities and entertainment at locations nearby, cliff top development in Trimingham looked a very dubious prospect indeed. The village, however, continues to grow, albeit slowly.

So, is Trimingham a singular village today? Anyone taking the trouble to stop will find that the people are the usual mix of locals and incomers, friendly enough and similar to folk elsewhere. And yet....

Trimingham itself makes no assertions. Other than many centuries ago when the local priests claimed to possess the head of St John the Baptist at the church, the village has never represented itself as unique or particularly remarkable.

Rev. R. C. Page was correct back in May 1919 when he stated that the parish was different from others in that nearly all of the inhabitants were tenants of J. H. Buxton and all owed him a lot. While it is undeniable that for much of the last century many of the residents of Trimingham benefited as tenants of the Buxton family and one or two other landholders, it is not unreasonable to wonder whether the village as a whole might not have been rather better served had it been less dependent on the views, decisions and interests of a few influential parties.

So, has Trimingham ever been a singular village?

Oh, I think so.

Bibliography

Association of RAF. *Norfolk 1939-45.*

Francis Blomefield. *History of Norfolk 1745.*

Laurie Brettingham. *Royal Air Force BEAM BENDERS No. 80 (Signals) Wing 1940-1945.* 1997

W. G. Clarke. *Norfolk and Suffolk.* 1921

David Duff. *Man of God.*

English Heritage. *RAF Trimingham, Norfolk.* Report by Wayne D. Cocroft.

J. P. Foynes. *The Battle of the East Coast (1939-1945).* 1994

Rebecca Fraser. *A People's History of Britain.*

E. A. Goodwin. *Cromer Past.*

Jane Hales. *Winds of Change in Norfolk.* 1984

Kenneth Hipper. *Smugglers All.*

Cyril Crawford Holden. *Cromer-The Cutting of the Gem.* 1967

R. S. Joby. *Regional Railway Handbooks No 2 - East Anglia.* 1987

Constance Rothery. *Poppyland Story,* and *The Poppyland Flyer - The Story of the Railway Line from Cromer to North Walsham 1906-1953.'* 1984

Norfolk Century. Eastern Counties Newspaper Group Ltd.

Roll-of-Honour.com 2002

A. C. Savin. *History of Cromer.* 1937

William Tylney Spurdens M.A. *Manuscript Collection relating to the County of Norfolk.* 1853.

1998-2002 *Subterranea Britannica*

Ward Lock & Co.

White's Directories.

Tom Williamson. *The Origins of Norfolk.* 1993

R. J. Wyatt. *Death from the Skies.* 1990

David Yaxley. *Portrait of Norfolk.* 1977

Acknowledgements

I would like to thank the many people who helped me so generously in the writing of this book. All provided information; some gave or lent material. All were interested, supportive, encouraging and willingly gave their time. My particular thanks are due to the following:-

Archant Photographic for photographs
Ron Banks, for information, maps and diagrams.
John Barker, for information and material about the church.
Diane Barnes and Martin Collingwood, for access to deeds and anecdotal material.
Nick Catford, for plans and photographs.
Julie Chance, for making much material and her home available for research. Also for many cups of coffee and memorable bacon sandwiches.
Edward Harrison, for anecdotal material and a guided tour.
Patrick and June Carpmael, for anecdotal material, copies of photographs and a map.
Bruce Hogg, for information about clearance of the minefield.
Anthony Kirk, for anecdotal and other information.
Penny Kirk, for the loan of photographs, postcards and pottery.
Simon Knott, for photographs.
Jack and Grace Olley, for anecdotal material and the loan of *Man of God*.
Geoffrey Pardon, for anecdotal material and making available photographs, postcards and newspaper cuttings.
Eric Reading, for anecdotal material and photographs.
Alec and Margaret Reynolds, for anecdotal material and photographs.
Alan and Daphne Self, for anecdotal material and photographs.

Thanks are also due to the following for their interest, encouragement and their various contributions:- Evelyn Collishaw, Bernard Francis, Adrian Kerr, Norfolk County Council, Norfolk Heritage Centre at Norfolk and Norwich Millennium Library, Norfolk Record Office, North Norfolk District Council, North Walsham Historical Society, Rachel Parkin, Peter & Lynda Siddall, Leslie Stean.